INVISIBLE WALLS

and

TO REMEMBER IS TO HEAL

INVISIBLE WALLS

A German Family under the Nuremberg Laws

Translated from the German by
John Brownjohn

AND

TO REMEMBER IS TO HEAL

Encounters between Victims of the Nuremberg Laws

Translated from the German by
John A. Broadwin

INGEBORG HECHT

NORTHWESTERN UNIVERSITY PRESS

Evanston, Illinois

Northwestern University Press
Evanston, Illinois 60208-4210

Invisible Walls originally published in German under the title *Als Unsichtbare Mauern wuchsen.* Copyright © 1984 by Hoffmann und Campe Verlag, Hamburg. English translation copyright © 1985 by Harcourt Brace Jovanovich, Inc. *To Remember Is to Heal* originally published in German under the title *Von der Heilsamkeit des Erinnerns: Opfer der Nürnberger Gesetze begegnen sich.* Copyright © 1991 by Hoffmann und Campe Verlag, Hamburg. English translation copyright © 1999 by Northwestern University Press. Published 1999.
All rights reserved.

Printed in the United States of America

ISBN 0-8101-1371-6

Library of Congress Cataloging-in-Publication Data

Hecht, Ingeborg.
    [Als unsichtbare Mauern wuchsen. English]
    Invisible walls : a German family under the Nuremberg laws / Ingeborg Hecht ; translated from the German by John Brownjohn ; & To remember is to heal : encounters between victims of the Nuremberg laws / Ingeborg Hecht ; translated from the German by John A. Broadwin.
        p. cm. — (Jewish lives)
    Previously published (1st work): 1st ed. San Diego : Harcourt Brace Jovanovich, c1985.
    ISBN 0-8101-1371-6 (paper)
    1. Hecht, Ingeborg. 2. Jews—Germany—Hamburg—Biography. 3. Children of interfaith marriage—Germany—Hamburg—Biography. 4. Jews—Germany—History—1933–1945. 5. Holocaust, Jewish (1933–1945)—Germany—Hamburg—Personal narratives. 6. Holocaust survivors—Germany. 7. Holocaust, Jewish (1939–1945)—Germany—Influence. 8. Hamburg (Germany)—Ethnic relations. I. Hecht, Ingeborg. Von der Heilsamkeit des Erinnerns. English. II. Title. III. Title: To remember is to heal. IV. Series
DS135.G5H34413 1999
943'.515004924'00922—dc21
[B]   99-11016
                                                       CIP

CONTENTS

INVISIBLE WALLS

A German Family under the Nuremberg Laws

TO REMEMBER IS TO HEAL
Encounters between Victims of the Nuremberg Laws

INVISIBLE WALLS

A German Family under the Nuremberg Laws

DEDICATED TO THE MEMORY OF MY PARENTS—
but written also for my grandsons Matthias and Florian,
whose mother, Barbara, left us in 1977

AUTHOR'S NOTE

LEAFING THROUGH *Das Sonderrecht für die Juden im NS-Staat** was almost like watching a rerun of my early life, half a century after the event. So many aspects of the Third Reich have already been explored that I propose to pick out one theme only—one that has hitherto escaped attention, save in Ralph Giordano's novel *Die Bertinis*, which came out when my manuscript was already complete and on its way to a publisher. My subject is the life of "half-breeds," or "offspring of privileged mixed marriages," in Nazi Germany.

Members of the younger generation are unfamiliar with these abstruse terms and verbal inventions; besides, they have problems of their own. Partly in tribute to those of this persecuted group who died, however, and partly as a contribution

---

**Das Sonderrecht für die Juden im NS-Staat* (Special Legislation for Jews in the National Socialist State. A Compilation of Measures and Directives, Their Content and Significance), edited by Joseph Walk, with contributions by Robert M. Kempner and Adalbert Rückert (Heidelberg/Karlsruhe: C. F. Müller Juristischer Verlag, 1981). The decrees cited here may be found, together with relevant references, on the pages indicated.

to the study of modern history, I think it appropriate to document their sufferings.

I have tried to abstain from all personal comments, speculations, complaints, and accusations. This was not easy, least of all in a world where inadmissible comparisons with other, more recent, atrocities are commonplace.

Speaking of comparisons, I have sometimes heard it argued that Hitler made a lot of "Aryan" Germans suffer, too—soldiers and their families, for instance. True, but they suffered as members of the "national community," enjoyed respect and mutual assistance. Their common enemy in battle spoke a different language.

Not so the persecuted, who were treated with scorn, contempt, and unfeeling hostility by people whose language was the same as theirs, and whose community they had belonged to—as fellow Germans—until 1933. The persecuted had to endure suffering as outcasts.

A final word on the subject of the "Special Legislation" decrees. Some of them read so absurdly that one is tempted to burst out laughing, but unintentional comedy on the part of murderers is no laughing matter.

Freiburg, Fall 1983

THE FAMILIES
(1883 – 1933)

3.24.38: *Jews are not permitted to consult public records except for genealogical purposes and for the study of Jewish folklore. In cases where the said exceptions apply, it must be ensured that the Jewish user of records is given access only to documents essential to the object of his investigation or research. (P. 219)*

I FOUND PARTICULARS of my ancestry, complete with names and details of social status, in a document case left behind by my father. That I possess these papers at all, neatly filed and photocopied (the originals were destroyed by fire), I owe to the period when Jewish lawyers could no longer style themselves attorneys, only "legal consultants," and were forbidden to have other than Jewish clients. That left my father with little work and a lot of time on his hands. The sole purpose for which he was still permitted to set foot in his old professional haunt, the Civil Justice Building on Sievekingsplatz, was to carry out genealogical research and photocopy what he unearthed there.

On September 24, 1883, a son, Felix, was born to the Jewish businessman Jakob Hecht and his wife Hanna, née Calmann, in the Harvestehude district of Hamburg. Felix was the eldest of five children belonging to a German family that would later be declared German no longer.

On April 23, 1900, a daughter, Edith, was born to Police Superintendent Friedrich von Sillich, a Protestant, and his

3

wife Fredegonde, née Ossenkopp, at Harburg an der Elbe. Edith was the scion of a good, solid German family that would later be termed "Aryan."

Friedrich von Sillich, a captain in the Royal Prussian Army Reserve, was last stationed at the headquarters of the 103rd Infantry Division's field recruiting depot in Meiningen. He died at Sains-Richaumont on April 12, 1918, of a heart attack following an air raid.

Jakob Hecht died at Hamburg in the same year.

Edith von Sillich's childhood was a happy one. As a five-year-old attired in a quaint little sailor outfit, she had good reason to feel proud of her papa when the kaiser visited Harburg in 1905—at 4:40 P.M. on June 19, to be precise—because "he was escorted on his progress through the town by Police Inspector von Sillich, likewise riding in an automobile." Thus the *Harburger Anzeiger*, which even printed a photograph of the occasion.

On Sundays and holidays the family would drive by wagonette to Harburg's "Schwarze Berge," there to lunch at one of the pleasant inns in the woods; or promenade down to the Old Harbor, that little gateway to the world near its mighty Hamburg neighbor, to which it was still linked by steam ferry; or stroll across the majestic Elbe Bridge. Harburg was Prussian in those days, and had yet to be incorporated in Hamburg.

As Edith grew older, she would roam the surrounding hills with her girlfriends and sing to the strains of brightly beribboned guitars. Riding was another of her pastimes, inexpensively pursued on a rather decrepit military charger belonging to Harburg's police force, which her father commanded. On Sundays she would attend St. Paul's Church and sing "Ein' feste Burg ist unser Gott," though its third verse . . . "If the world were filled with devils"—had yet to assume any topical

4

significance. She also knew the synagogue on the corner of Eissendorferstrasse and Knoopstrasse, a place of worship frequented by members of a different religion to which no stigma then attached. Jews had lived in Harburg since 1610, under a charter granted them by William, duke of Braunschweig-Lüneburg.

I mention these things because my mother, pretty little Edith von Sillich, who grew up in a snug, friendly environment dedicated to probity and good faith, never quite grasped what befell her after little more than ten years of marriage.

The von Sillichs of Harburg were enthusiastic collectors of pewter, which they used to buy at the Rembrandthaus, the Hechts' antique shop in the Colonnades at Hamburg, though only on a modest scale because an army captain's pay was meager, and there were debts incurred as a lieutenant to be deducted from it.

Felix Hecht, the proprietor's son, who was sixteen years older than Edith, occasionally helped her with her homework.

When war broke out, Edith volunteered for service as a kitchen and ward auxiliary at the Duke of Meiningen Hospital. She had never intended to become a nurse, but the fatherland had summoned all good citizens to do their patriotic duty. An opportunity to continue this budding career occurred when her father died, so she transferred to a school of nursing in Berlin. In 1919, shortly before she completed her training, Felix Hecht asked her to marry him.

The ceremony took place on May 25, 1920, at "Villa Hanna," otherwise known as No. 7, Frauenthal, near the Alster, with a pastor and a cantor in attendance. That evening everyone celebrated at the Winterhuder Fährhaus and posed for a grand family photograph.

The bridal pair had embarked on what came to be known as a "privileged mixed marriage."

I was born on April 1, 1921, in a private clinic owned by Dr. Adolf Calmann, my grandmother Hanna's brother, at No. 68, Johnsallee. My brother Wolfgang was born two years later, on November 11, 1923.

The Nazi authorities were to coin a special term for the likes of us: "first degree half-breeds." It was for us, whom they ceased to regard as German citizens, that they devised the bulk of the so-called Nuremberg Laws "for the protection of German blood and German honor."

No. 7, Frauenthal, named Villa Hanna after my beautiful grandmother, was a handsome corner house with a gabled roof, a portico, and a front garden. It was the one house in this small street in Hamburg's former monastic quarter that did not survive the war. Today its site is occupied by a gas station.

Villa Hanna was situated in Harvestehude, one of the city's finest residential districts, where town houses were adorned with Jugendstil porticoes, neoclassical windows and balconies, neobaroque gables, imposing Wilhelminian façades, and other architectural embellishments typical of the age of German industrial expansion. In the midst of this desirable area was Eichenpark, where we used to feed the swans on the Alster.

The Hecht grandparents and their five children were fortunate to live in Harvestehude. Their forebears had come from the Yiddish-speaking ghettos of Eastern Europe, a vanished world known to us only through the books of Joseph Roth, Isaac B. Singer, and Manès Sperber. Destroyed by deportation and extermination, its sole memorial a few old photographic records, it has passed into history.

But my grandparents were no longer part of that world.

Not until it was engulfed by the common experience of suffering in Auschwitz, Maidanek, Treblinka, and Warsaw were the eastern and western children of Israel reminded of their common roots.

As they relaxed in the handsome garden of their Frauenthal mansion, or on its terrace, which must have been little less spacious than an entire house in one of the eastern ghettos, these "western" Jews were able to forget and dismiss the tribulations of their race—but only very briefly. It was not until the middle of the nineteenth century, or 1864, that Jews were at long last granted full citizenship; only a generation later, they were brutally ostracized once more.

The eldest son, my father, was made to study law. His real love was ancient languages, but Grandfather Hecht wanted a business manager. As things turned out, he might just as well have dispensed with one. . . .

The two younger brothers, Hellmuth and Edgar, were earmarked to take over the family firm and become art dealers. (Hellmuth later emigrated to Quito and became a monk, and nothing more was ever heard of him.) A third brother died in Hamburg at a very early age—the only member of his generation (discounting the monk, one presumes) to have died a natural death. Aunt Alice, a polio victim with a permanent limp, moved to Berlin and ran the Tauentzienstrasse branch of the family firm until it was driven out of business.

In 1927 my father decided to quit the shelter of Grandmother Hanna's luxurious but matriarchal abode. Cashing in his patrimony, he used it to purchase No. 73, Hochallee, a house typical of the area bounded by Klosterstern and Innocentiastrasse. It had a modest neoclassical frontage but none of the ornamentation and architectural flamboyance of tree-lined Frauenthal.

Here Wolfgang and I grew up, and here we went to school, I to a private junior high school for girls in nearby Mittelweg, he to a primary school in Schlüterstrasse. It was in this "respectable" neighborhood between Jungfrauenthal and Hallerstrasse that we played Indians and trappers, learned to bicycle in the then almost traffic-free streets, and hauled our toboggans to Innocentia Park. Our back garden boasted a pear tree big enough to clamber around in—quite an adventure for city-bred children—and a sand pit in which we dug a sort of cavern lined with planks and shrouded in blankets. This was where we smoked pipes of peace—imaginary ones, of course—in the company of Lux the German shepherd, Blacky the cat, and a neighbor's son from nearby Parkallee, who played with us until he joined the Hitler Youth. But we weren't allowed to sleep in the open like the boy next door, whose enviably romantic privilege it was to camp outside with his father for a whole week after Yom Kippur, the Day of Atonement, in memory of the Israelites' trek through the desert. In accordance with religious tradition, which prescribed that the stars should be visible through the roof of their bivouac, they slept in a "tabernacle" of woven twigs. They didn't do this "just for fun," our parents assured us, but our ignorance of Jewish customs extended to the menorah in Father's study, which we simply regarded as a candlestick with seven branches.

Although our parents belonged to different religions, and it was intended that we should someday choose our own, we were told nothing about Judaism. This, I suppose, was an aid to the assimilation to which most "western" Jews aspired.

After we had spent five years as "children from a good home," complete with cook and nursemaid, our parents filed for divorce. Their divorce, which was granted in 1933, had nothing to do with the ominous political situation, nor did they ever quarrel in our presence. They parted for purely personal reasons and on genuinely good terms, as my mother repeatedly demonstrated with a courage and fortitude that later put her own life in danger. One immediate token of this was her refusal to allow my father, who wasn't the most practical of men, to look for another place to live. For the time being, we all remained under the same roof.

PROFESSIONAL WORRIES
AND DOMESTIC UPHEAVALS
(1934–1938)

1.16.34: *Professional contact with attorneys whose license has been revoked, inter alia when revoked on account of non-Aryan descent, is prohibited. This prohibition also extends to the sharing of office facilities, leasings. . . . All sharing of office facilities and professional association between Aryan and non-Aryan attorneys . . . is prohibited. (P. 68)*

12.20.34: *Former attorneys may no longer style themselves "attorney." (P. 100)*

12.19.35: *The courts must ensure that Jews are not designated as public defenders, court-appointed counsel, bankruptcy trustees, and the like. (P. 147)*

BY THE EARLY SUMMER of 1933, decrees and directives like the following had reared their heads everywhere, and the attitude they exemplified was steadily hardening.

5.17.33: *Medicaments of Jewish manufacture are to be prescribed only when other preparations of the same standard are unobtainable. (P. 23)*

6.30.33: *National Socialists are forbidden to enter premises frequented by Jews. This applies only to cafés and restaurants, not to hotels. (P. 34)*

5.9.33: *All municipal employees are requested to desist from patronizing Jewish stores, and to cancel existing monthly credit accounts forthwith. (P. 21)*

The logical effect of these measures was something we still remember as "the boycott."

On April 1, my twelfth birthday, SA storm troopers stationed themselves outside every Jewish store in Hamburg (and

13

elsewhere) and tried to dissuade shoppers from entering. "This is a Jewish-owned business," they announced. "Didn't you know?" Though rather bemused and surprised, plenty of townsfolk were sufficiently unintimidated—at that juncture—to run the Brownshirts' gauntlet and go inside. The situation was too novel and absurd, too unwonted and sudden an encroachment on their daily lives, for them to take a serious view of the threat and what it portended. The very few people to take it seriously were those who had read *Mein Kampf*. After all, Hitler had made no secret of the ruthlessness with which he intended to execute his grand design.

Having found a silver five-mark piece among my birthday presents, I decided to spend a small proportion of my wealth on some chocolate eggs. Outside the local candy store, the men in brown said their piece. My "Jewish kinship" was not apparent—according to the Nazis, all Jews had hooked noses!—so I proudly brushed past them. (At that early stage we could still afford to look proud of our daring; later on, we took such risks with a pounding heart. . . .) The longtime owners of the candy store, two little old ladies, were red-eyed with weeping. I got my chocolate eggs and a marzipan egg as a bonus.

An announcement published the following April gave some indication of how the fatherland proposed to reward its Jewish sons for services rendered:

4.19.34:   *According to the* Hamburger Fremdenblatt, *the Aryan Clause applies to all organizations affiliated to the Central Committee of Hamburg's civic associations. Non-Aryan members are to be expelled by 5.15.34. (P. 78)*

I don't know if my father was due for expulsion, but he certainly didn't wait to find out. He had been a member of the

14

Greater Hamburg Home Guard, Harvestehude District—in other words, an auxiliary policeman—since 1923.

The laws affecting my father's profession came into being before he had really managed to get his practice off the ground, so they nipped his livelihood in the bud. My mother tried to keep the wolf from the door by converting our Hochallee home into a miniature boarding house.

Where our "Aryan" grandparents were concerned, Wolfgang and I occasionally dipped into the Almanach de Gotha, or directory of noble families. It transpired that the Sillichs had not been granted their coveted "von" until 1871. "True" aristocrats, most of whom could trace their lineage back to the Middle Ages, tended to look down their noses at such upstarts. Although we couldn't have cared less whether the "von" was ancient or modern, the little prefix now came in handy. Mother reverted to her maiden name so that "Aryans," too, need have no qualms about renting rooms from us—to begin with, at least—but it soon dawned on us children that our future mode of existence would be a frugal one. Mother had absolutely no idea how to run a boarding house. The place was managed on very haphazard lines, and all that kept our tenants content was the pleasant atmosphere that reigned there. The venture was doomed from the outset, and the strain told increasingly on our parents' state of health.

Domestic dramas were commonplace, most of our tenants being Jewish and under intense emotional pressure, so my father became a sort of unofficial divorce lawyer. One day we were told that Herr and Frau L. had decided to part. The wife and children were to emigrate, the husband would stay behind with us. Everything had been settled amicably, and there was even a farewell party. I can still hear the sentimental lyric blaring from the phonograph horn: "Reich mir zum Abschied noch einmal die Hände, / Goodnight, goodnight, good-nigh-eet. . . ." The ladies dabbed their eyes. Herr L. looked despondent. "From *Viktoria und ihr Husar*—how apt!" my father remarked with a ghost of a smile. The operetta was set in Hungary, and the attractive divorcée was about to join a Hungarian lover abroad. The margin between mawkishness and despair was slender indeed. . . .

But none of these legal tangles helped to improve our financial position, which continued to deteriorate. Having no reserves left to fall back on, my parents were forced to let their staff go.

My mother, though conscientious and courageous, was no businesswoman. On November 29, 1934, the Hochallee house was compulsorily sold at auction and we moved into an apartment at No. 27, Hagedornstrasse. Father came, too. Two of the apartment's six rooms were let to provide us with the barest basic income.

At the same time, Father was obliged to dissolve his partnership, give up his shared office, and dismiss the "Aryan" secretary who had been with him for years. She felt as bad about this as we did, and continued to pay us social calls for a long time to come. Father took a much smaller office in the Hamburger Hof, on Jungfernstieg, and employed a Jewish secretary for a few hours each week.

One of our rooms in Hagedornstrasse was let to a married couple, both of whom were half-Jewish. The young wife, Manon, became like an elder sister to me. She later moved back to Berlin, her native city, where I happened to be staying with her on Kristallnacht, the "Night of Broken Glass." The other rented room was occupied by a Jewish chemist from London, Dr. Herbert Weil, who was working at Hamburg University. Both of them subsequently testified to the postwar Reparations Office that we were still, at this time, in possession of "intact, middle-class household effects." Such were the lengths to which one was driven in the 1950s by officialdom's strange insistence on proof that was almost impossible to obtain. . . .

The apartment was, in fact, quite well appointed in a way that recalled my grandparents' luxurious establishment on Frauenthal, though the furniture was beginning to fall apart. We did not, however, have enough to live on. After school I acted as baby-sitter for five precious marks a week—a rather unusual sideline in those days, and one I heartily disliked.

But even this apartment, with its faded elegance, its balcony and garden, was not to be ours for long. In 1937 we moved again, this time to Hansastrasse, where we took an apartment somewhat at odds with our customary way of life. We shared the place with a couple whom we had never met before. Herr S. and his wife—he was a baker—occupied one and a half rooms; we occupied the remaining three and a half. It was, to say the least, an unfamiliar situation.

This time Father did not accompany us. He stayed behind in Hagedornstrasse with his younger brother Edgar, who, together with Aunt Hanna and cousin Hans, had been our neighbor there. Edgar's existing tenant, an "Aryan" art dealer named Alfred Lawrenz, or "Ali" for short, made room for Father by moving in with us. This was a blessing. Ali proved a great source of help in the dark days ahead. But for him, we should not have survived the coming years so relatively unscathed.

THE "COMRADES"
(1934–1936)

8.17.34: *Young persons belonging to Jewish youth clubs, who do not participate in State Youth Day, may go hiking on Sundays but are not permitted to engage in athletics. (P. 89)*

10.8.35: *Hostels constructed or still to be constructed by Jewish youth clubs will henceforth bear the designation "Jewish overnight centers," not "Jewish youth hostels." (P. 135)*

IN 1934 A SCHOOL FRIEND roped me into the "German Jewish Comrades' Hiking Association." This club sported a smart pennant—a white seagull on a blue background—and a snappy marching song: "Comrades one and all are we, decent types we aim to be. . . ."

It was through the association that I got to know "Little Inge" (a nickname that differentiates her from my lanky self to this day), whose fate will accompany me through these pages as it has throughout my life. Our name was popular in those days, not least with assimilated Jews, because it sounded so irreproachably Nordic. Little Inge was fair-haired and blue-eyed, which made her an exception in our group. "And she claims to be half-Jewish!" said one of the boys when she first turned up. "Hitler and Goebbels would be madly envious of your 'master race' looks." We were becoming adept at black humor, and Little Inge's appearance gave rise to a lot of tragicomic incidents.

For two years we spent our Sundays and vacations tramping through the hills outside Harburg and southward across the Lüneburger Heide to Hittfeld, Buchholz, and Müden.

Because we didn't regard ourselves as a specifically "Jewish" association, we ventured into youth hostels—not always without a trace of uneasiness—and joined other hikers in the dining hall or around the campfire until our beloved club was disbanded in 1936.

Evening meetings were held once a week. It was some time before our parents gathered, from certain out-of-character remarks and snippets of jargon, that our group leaders had begun to subject us to "sociopolitical" indoctrination. Actually, it bored us stiff when they felt duty-bound to read us extracts from *Das Kapital,* and well-meant exegeses of Marxism from older comrades did little to set us on the leftward road, though we naturally shared their devotion to justice for the oppressed of this world. Our unfortunate parents were now doubly afraid, however, not that we would develop Red Front tendencies, but that our association might be branded Communist as well as Jewish and hounded in consequence.

The hitchhiking and singing we enjoyed. Hitchhiking was a far less common mode of travel than it is today—far less potentially dangerous, too. We always hitchhiked as a group, cadging rides from friendly truck drivers and bellowing our songs into the wind, which made the white seagull on our blue pennant flap and flutter overhead. To good little middle-class girls, it all seemed the height of adventure. Despite the ludicrous decree of August 17, 1934, we also took part in field sports and scouting. For once, I wasn't too annoyed with the authors of such bizarre edicts, because I found violent physical exertion in the woods and fields intolerable as well as unnecessary. "Growing too fast for her heart to cope" was the verdict of "Uncle Dr. Zacharias," our longtime family physician and friend, when swimming proved to be the only sport I could stand.

It should here be added that Dr. Zacharias was deported

to Theresienstadt on July 15, 1942. I came across one last, pathetic reminder of him in Käthe Starke's book *Der Führer schenkt den Juden eine Stadt*, which appeared in 1975. Having contracted typhus, he took his own life. "He had chosen not to wait until malnutrition completed its work. In view of prevailing conditions, he put an end to himself. On August 11, 1942, three weeks after his arrival, this gifted physician . . . and expert diagnostician made his own diagnosis and acted on it by taking a drug he had brought with him."

On Mondays we waged verbal warfare with the BDM [German Girls' League] members in our class. Half the pupils in our school were Jewish, and since friendships were still unaffected by racial mania, our debates did not assume a very dramatic form. After all, we sang the same songs in praise of the great outdoors, with their allusions to sun, wind, and stars. Only the very latest brand of doggerel failed to appeal to us: "As the golden sun of evening / Sent its last rays slanting down, / One of Hitler's regiments / Marched into a little town. . . ." Pity to spoil a good tune, we thought.

In 1936 the Comrades' Hiking Association was banned. The Zionists among us, well aware that there was only one place on earth where a Jewish community could try to find peace, were all for emigrating to Palestine. The Communists wanted to stay, if possible. Arrested and detained for some time, our group leader was released before long because his family had hurriedly made arrangements for him to emigrate. However, we now knew what a concentration camp was. . . .

Little Inge and I were the only girl comrades left. Our fathers, having fought for Germany in the war, were deluded enough to bank on the gratitude of a country that had disowned them. Decrees like the one below show just how mean and cynical the authorities could be when they chose:

7.13.36:   *Concessionary telephone calls for war-blinded veterans will not be granted to non-Aryans. (P. 168)*

Though keen on sports, unlike me, my brother Wolfgang was soon expelled from the Hamburg Athletic Club (HSV)—a blow from which he took a long time to recover.

His enthusiasm for football had prompted him to hitchhike to Berlin for the 1936 Olympics. This was a rare mode of travel, as I have already said, and thirteen-year-olds were not as sophisticated as they are today, but my parents, who could not afford to pay his fare, had neither the heart nor the strength of mind to deny him such an important and exceptional treat.

Nazi opportunism during the games was reflected in confidential directives like these:

6.11.35:   *Notices reading "Jews Unwelcome" and the like are to be unobtrusively removed (on account of the Olympic Games) from all main thoroughfares. (P. 117)*

12.3.35:   *To avoid jeopardizing the 1936 Olympic Games in Berlin, all anti-Jewish placards and posters in the vicinity of Garmisch-Partenkirchen, where the Winter Games will be held, are to be removed. (P. 143)*

My brother also had religious interests and commitments. He belonged to the "Vereinigung 1937" [1937 Confraternity], originally registered as the "Reichsverband nichtarischer Christen" [National Association of Non-Aryan Christians] and later as the "Paulusbund" [League of St. Paul]. The Paulusbund, too, organized excursions and hiking tours and held evening get-togethers, but the Gestapo had to be notified of all such meetings in advance. This was less an incentive than a deterrent, and the league was banned before the outbreak of war.

The thwarting of Wolfgang's enthusiasms, religious and athletic, made life almost more difficult for him than it was for me. As the forcible estrangement of "Aryans" and "non-Aryans" proceeded with awful inevitability, so more and more mental conflicts arose. Wolfgang became very silent, very withdrawn, and this was bound to affect his outlook on life.

SCHOOL DAYS

(1935–1937)

9.15.35: Law for the Preservation of German Blood and German Honor

1. Marriages between Jews and nationals of German or kindred stock are prohibited. Marriages contracted despite this are null and void.

2. Extramarital intercourse between Jews and nationals of German or kindred stock is prohibited.

3. Jews may not employ in their households female nationals of German or kindred stock aged less than forty-five years. (P. 127)

9.15.35: Reich Citizenship Law

Only nationals of German or kindred stock are citizens of the Reich. Political rights are vested in Reich citizens alone. (P. 127)

11.14.35: Executive Order Pertaining to the Reich Citizenship Law

Jews (i.e., persons descended from at least three racially full-Jewish grandparents, full-Jewish being taken to mean belonging to the Jewish religious community, or half-breeds with two full-Jewish grandparents . . .) cannot be citizens of the Reich, have no right of political franchise, and may not hold public office. . . . The Führer can grant exemption from these regulations. (P. 139)

My brother and I were twelve and fourteen years old respectively when the Nuremberg Laws were promulgated, so we had at least some idea of what they meant. My realization of the terrible fears they must have aroused in my parents, whose "privileged mixed marriage" had produced two "half-breeds," I owe to Lotte Paepcke, who presented me with a copy of her book *Ich wurde vergessen* when it was published in 1970. Born at Freiburg in 1910, she qualified as a lawyer in 1933 but was then debarred from practicing, either independently or at the university.

4.6.33:   Junior Staff Regulation

> *The filling of junior faculty posts with members of the Jewish race is prohibited; existing contracts of employment with such persons must not be extended or renewed. (P. 11)*

Lotte Paepcke was shielded from further danger by her marriage to an "Aryan" scientist, but not indefinitely. When her position became precarious, she went into hiding in a Freiburg convent. To begin with, however, she and her family lived in Leipzig. Their neighbors in the apartment house there, who had to be informed of her status, accepted her and were not unfriendly toward this "mixed" couple, whom they regarded as faintly exotic, but the price that had to be paid for their goodwill was high indeed.

"I cleaned the stairs and corridors with the utmost diligence . . . and greeted all those strangers in an affable, ingratiating manner. There it was again, looming over me, the curse that weighed so heavy on the persecuted: the need to beg for benevolence. . . ."

For her life between two worlds was a mosaic composed of fragments which, when put together, could not be other than a picture of self-effacing discretion. She puts it this way:

"You had to bamboozle all the people you encountered into liking you, so as to disarm them in an emergency. You had to work on them surreptitiously so that, whatever happened, their compassion would be primed and ready, for example, to mitigate the lust for hatred ordained by the authorities."

Although the other tenants had accepted Lotte Paepcke and her family, a member of the Nazi women's association was detailed to "ensure that the Jewess behaves decently, see that she causes the neighbors no offense, and note her associates." One need hardly point out how easy it would have been for someone living in an apartment house to wrangle with a neighbor over some trifle and thus "cause offense," but the persecuted cannot afford such luxuries. "The outcast's weapon was to be likeable."

Lotte Paepcke's son Peter presented an even more dramatic problem. He was eight years old.

"When his father entered him for the relevant primary school, the headmaster, a holder of the Nazi 'Blood Order,' did not disguise his reluctance to admit a half-breed. Although

Peter was debarred from a secondary education, however, the primary school was obliged to accept him. So he was duly subjected to German discipline, coming to attention and saluting every morning when the monitor reported that Class IIIb had 'fallen in' for lessons, and marching around with the others in rank and file during break. Only the monitor at their head was entitled to salute assistant teachers, whereas the headmaster had to be smartly saluted by everyone in the school. Peter learned that the Führer never slept a wink, so great was his concern for his people, and that Jews should be struck whenever one came across them. He communicated this advice to us at supper one evening. The blood rushed to my head, I was so appalled by the enormity of the moment and my inability to say, 'Look, here's a Jew sitting right in front of you— your own mother!' But the boy was still so childish and naïve and so inclined to blurt out everything he knew that we didn't dare enlighten him. . . . I was filled with shame. My life was becoming diseased with simulated friendliness, breaking out in sores produced by the bacillus of insincerity. Many were the nights when I debated whether to wield the scalpel and come clean, with the child and everyone else. Any such operation was bound to be fatal, however, and I was driven to conclude that it would be more courageous to go on enduring the pain of dishonesty with a view to saving the whole situation. And so I felt myself taking on the look in the eye, the obsequious smile, that has accompanied the Jews on their millennial progress through the lives of alien peoples."

Unlike me, Little Inge can recall exactly when she first heard of the Nuremberg Laws. She was with her class at Vogelkoje, the school's vacation hostel on the island of Sylt.

"One night we were all instructed to assemble in the dining hall. Some Nazi bigwig was sounding off on the radio—Goeb-

31

bels, I think. He was proclaiming the 'Nuremberg Laws.' I heard, 'For the preservation of German blood and German honor . . .' We weren't really concentrating, and would much sooner have been doing something else. My form mistress, Fräulein Riecke (who's still alive and has always been a resolute anti-Fascist), became more and more edgy. After pacing up and down, she paused behind my chair. As though by chance, she rested one hand on my shoulder, then momentarily stroked my hair. I was rather puzzled, because I hadn't grasped the significance of the announcement and the extent to which it would affect my future, my whole life. That wasn't made clear to me until I got home. My parents were waiting for me at the station, and my father, who was usually so cheerful and full of fun, greeted me with a funereal expression."

There were BDM girls in Little Inge's class, too.

"After the Sylt trip, one or two of them started making remarks about my 'non-Aryan' ancestry. When Fräulein Riecke heard this, she asked me to leave the classroom a moment. Then she impressed on the others that I didn't belong to one 'side' or the other—that I'd fallen between two stools, so they must treat me fairly and decently, not cut the ground from under my feet. My classmates were impressed by her powers of persuasion. The rest of the teachers at our school were also firmly opposed to Hitler, so I was able to complete my final year and take my junior high school diploma with a pleasurable sense of security, surrounded by loyal friends with whom I still keep in touch to this day. I wasn't allowed to take my university entrance examination, but that would have been financially impossible in any case, because my father—he was a leather merchant, and no 'Aryan' firm could do business with him—was finding it harder and harder to make a living.

"Shortly before the junior diploma exam in April 1937, our class began to receive sporadic visits from officials sent by the high school inspectorate. One of these preliminary oral examinations was in English, a subject I excelled at, so I often got asked questions. At the staff meeting afterward, the official asked Fräulein Riecke who I was, describing me as 'that archetype of the Aryan race.' With the greatest relish, she informed him that I was the only 'half-Jewess' in her class."

Inge's sister Ursula, who was four years younger, fared less well. She had to leave the Emilie Wüstenfeld School after only two years because it was scheduled to be made "Jew-free," so she failed to complete her education. Strangely enough, though, she was deemed worthy of employment in an "Aryan" household during her year's compulsory national service. Then, after attending a private business college, she went to work in an office. This meant that she had, by a roundabout route, ended up in a job as good as we, with our junior high school diplomas, could still hope to obtain.

From 1927 onward I had attended the Ria Wirth School, a private establishment on Mittelweg. We were in the fifth year when Fräulein Angerstein became our form mistress. The need to impart "National Socialist ideas" wrought an inevitable change in the teaching of her two special subjects, German and history. We greatly admired her, however, and I was saddened rather than angered by her habit of wearing a swastika pin in her blouse. Perhaps it was her way of forestalling any official rebukes for her willingness to teach at so racially mixed a school.

Aware that I enjoyed writing and reading, but that I prided myself on the length of my German compositions, Fräulein Angerstein taught me that brevity is the soul of wit. She showed me how an author could be both discursive and "masterly" by introducing me to the works of Adalbert Stifter. We read *Brigitta* together, and she also presented me with a copy of *Abdias*.

One day she asked me why I didn't attend one of the so-called national-political classes at which pupils were familiarized with "the Germany of today," adding, "You're just as much half-Aryan as half-Jewish, aren't you?" So I turned up, just for once, and heard my intelligent, well-respected teacher spouting Nazi slogans. Did she really believe such rubbish, I wondered? Well, even if I couldn't skip the ridiculous daily "flag parades" in the little school yard, I could at least pass that up.

7.30.34: *Exemption of non-Aryan pupils from attendance at weekly classes in "National Socialist ideas" (national political instruction) held on Saturdays for pupils who do not belong to the Hitler Youth. Non-Aryan pupils are to be excused from these on request. (P. 87)*

Our headmistress joined the NS-Frauenschaft [National Socialist Women's Association] and started to treat her Jewish and half-Jewish pupils with a certain aloofness. This, too, may have been a form of protective camouflage, because she never asked any of them to leave. She did need fee-paying parents, of course, but I shall always be grateful to her for granting me a scholarship during my latter years at the school, when we could no longer meet the substantial cost of a private education. If she sometimes saw fit to point out that my special circumstances obliged me to make a special effort, showing little awareness of the childish distress occasioned by such a sense of obligation, this was only secondary to the problem I shared with so many other girls: how were we supposed to concentrate in school when things were so bad at home?

Elisabeth Flügge, a teacher whose subjects included German, local studies, geography, mathematics, botany, and zoology, was made of different stuff. Employed at the school

34

since 1926, she steadfastly refused to trim her sails to the winds of change. With a courage that only her contemporaries can fully appreciate, she devoted herself to the welfare, not only of her bewildered and apprehensive pupils, but also of their gravely endangered parents. She never forgot the occasion in 1933 when one of her girls timidly inquired, "Are *Jewish* children allowed to go collecting, too?" It was a reasonable question, given the hordes of children, both in and out of Hitler Youth uniform, who infested the sidewalks with coin boxes in their hands. In those days, everyone was collecting from everyone else for every conceivable form of charity (Winter Relief Fund, Mother and Child Fund) and on every possible occasion (e.g., "Stewpot Sundays," when the German housewife was officially encouraged to serve up a simple, one-course meal and put the money she saved in a collecting box). Not unnaturally, Jewish children wanted to join in. They had yet to learn the meaning of isolation.

"When you take your girls on an outing," the headmistress had enjoined Frau Flügge, "be sure to put all the blondes in front."

When Jews became subject to a variety of travel restrictions—they were barred from sleepers and dining cars, could only travel third class, and found that many hotels and boarding houses either couldn't or wouldn't take them in—Frau Flügge rented a ten-room house at Ollsen in der Heide and vacationed there with her own two youngsters and a dozen Jewish children. I spent one vacation there myself, as I was recently reminded by her niece Ilse, a school friend of mine. "We swam in the Aue, picked blueberries, played theater," she wrote. "It was a lovely, lighthearted time, don't you remember?"

My memories of it are only vague—blurred and obscured by all the less lighthearted happenings at home. . . .

One day Frau Flügge heard from a Jewish lawyer that the mother of one of her pupils was to be deported. "So I went to the Gestapo with my knees knocking," she told an interviewer from the *Hamburger Abendblatt*. The Gestapo officer reminded her that she was addressing a public servant. "So are you," she retorted, and a miracle occurred. The man behind the desk poured out his heart to her. He'd always tried to do his honest duty, he said despairingly, but now—"Now I'm expected to compile death lists for that devil!" He removed Frau Flügge's protégée from his list, but a colleague later restored her name in line with Party directives.

Frau Flügge also managed to help would-be emigrants in a very special way. She persuaded Lady Oldfield of Cambridge, a friend of her daughter's and niece of Lord Balfour, the former prime minister, to provide affidavits—documents guaranteeing large sureties—for penniless Jews who would otherwise have been refused admission to many countries. Anyone in possession of such a document could consider himself saved.

One long-heralded decree was phrased as follows:

2.24.39:   Obligatory Relinquishment of Jewish-Owned Gems and Articles of Jewelry

> *In regard to the acquisition and purchase of such articles of precious metal, precious stones, and pearls as are to be surrendered by Jews, no offer may henceforth be declined by the same. . . . (P. 283)*

The obligation on Jews to surrender "valuables" of all kinds, including fur coats and objets d'art (the list, which later embraced typewriters, radios, and electrical appliances, was infinitely elastic!), made it hard for emigrants to support themselves in foreign countries, because they could take no money at all. Like other courageous Germans, Frau Flügge began to smuggle valuables abroad with the aid of a friend. On one occasion, jewelry secreted in the funnel of the *Monte Rosa*, a German passenger ship bound for Rio de Janeiro, was picked up there by its owners.

In this as in other respects, Elisabeth Flügge risked her life.

It would be facile to ask why so few—or, at any rate, too few—people summoned up the courage to help the victims of Nazi persecution more effectively. Speaking for myself, I know that I would never have done what Sophie and Hans Scholl, those young German resistance fighters of the White Rose movement, tried to do for all our sakes. They died in 1943, in the cause of freedom, and went to the gallows so bravely that even their jailers and executioners remarked on it.

I say this because the land of Israel has tried to show due gratitude. In the mountains near Jerusalem is the Avenue of the Just, and planted there for Elisabeth Flügge is a little carob tree. It commemorates her receipt of Israel's highest honor, the Yad Vashem medal and citation. Yad Vashem is also the name of the monument erected there in accordance with Isaiah 56:5: "Even unto them will I give in mine house and within my walls a place and a name. . . ." Many millions of stones make up its mosaic floor, one for each of those who were sent to concentration camps and murdered.

Elisabeth Flügge died in Hamburg on February 1, 1983.

Her diametrical opposite was our scripture teacher, a dapper, good-looking clergyman from a neighboring parish. My enthusiasm for the printed word earned me his benevolent interest and the proud privilege of reading aloud to the class.

Then, one day, I noticed that he had begun to ignore me. It wasn't long before I grasped the truth: he had discovered the "ancestry" of the girl he had so often invited to read from the New Testament. I never attended scripture class again.

3.13.35:   Segregation of Children of Non-Aryan Descent in Primary Schools

> *The establishment of separate Jewish primary schools is to be encouraged. The drafting of a law to this effect is in hand. To facilitate racial segregation, school authorities are to compile a statistical analysis of their pupils' racial affiliations. (P. 108)*

8.31.35:   *Prizes may not be awarded to non-Aryan pupils. (P. 125)*

In contrast to Little Inge and me, my brother Wolfgang suffered detriment and discrimination in primary school, and was denied the opportunity of moving to a junior high school after four years. In 1937 he became a clerical trainee, but he also contrived to attend a private night school and obtain his junior high school diploma—in defiance of discrimination, as it were. (After July 2, 1942, he would have required ministerial permission even for that.)

OUTLOOK UNCERTAIN
(1937–1938)

4.4.34: Restrictions on Attendance at Secondary Schools

Restrictions on the admission of non-Aryan pupils apply not only to secondary schools but also to junior high schools (pursuant to the law against overfilling German schools). As regards admission of non-Aryan pupils to these schools . . . preference must be given to pupils with a proven admixture of Aryan blood. . . . Children of Aryan descent may on no account be disadvantaged in favor of those of non-Aryan descent. (P. 76)

ALTHOUGH "LIMITED OPPORTUNITIES" for advancement existed on paper, it was effectively impossible for us, by the time I left school, to move from junior high schools to secondary, college preparatory schools. We were thus denied the chance to matriculate and go to the university. Older companions in misfortune were just able to graduate, if they had completed their courses by April 1934, but most of them were first required to prove that they would leave the country immediately afterward.

This put an end to my childhood dream, which was to follow in my father's footsteps and study law; in any case, his practice was scarcely worthy of the name by then. I had no time to wallow in despair, however. What mattered was to act fast, before any new regulation could be imposed, and decide on the best thing to do under the prevailing circumstances. If I couldn't be a lawyer, the profession I chose must at least involve the written word. Publishing? Journalism?

In the winter of 1936 my headmistress had sent me to the editorial offices of the *Hamburger Fremdenblatt* with an excellent German report and a letter of recommendation. After a pleas-

41

ant interview, I was offered a traineeship and given a questionnaire to complete. Elated, I sat down at a little table with pen poised. Then the truth dawned.

"Non-Aryans" were unacceptable. My previous knowledge of the Nuremberg Laws had been only theoretical, so to speak; now their evil, cruel reality was staring me in the face in black and white.

I left the newspaper office and walked across Rathausplatz, which had already been renamed in honor of Germany's great Leader. What pleasure could I take in the splendid neoclassical arcades beside the Kleine Alster—what pleasure could I take in the whole of this lovely, beloved city—if the sense of belonging was denied me? I envied the happy people in the motor launch chugging past below me on its way from Kehrwieder Canal to Jungfernstieg Bridge. With mingled sentimentality and earnestness, I wondered what life had left to offer me. But I never asked myself that question again. It was only later that I grasped how much I managed to endure for twelve long years, though always buoyed up by a feeling of happiness that I lived in Hamburg. I never wished to be anyone or anything else—not even "Aryan."

It was Easter 1937, and our final day at school had arrived. First came a rather emotional lesson with a school inspector listening in, then a speech about our going forth into the big, wide world, then the traditional program of entertainment staged by the class below ours. Then we all repaired to the classroom to make our farewells.

Most of the Jewish girls had already obtained passage on ships bound for freedom, though only after some anxious moments. I particularly recall Steffi Bernstein, a shipowner's daughter, who came to school looking tearful, day after day, because her father had been arrested. (The "Aryanization" of the Hamburg shipping lines plays a part in Arnold Zweig's documentary novel *The Axe of Wandsbek*.)

My "Aryan" classmates were in high spirits. Some of them were going on to senior schools, others entering the professions of their choice.

Neither of these things applied to me. I could neither emigrate nor train for a profession that appealed to me. My father had found me a probationary post with Gustav Weber, a patent attorney with offices at No. 11, Rathausmarkt, but the very term "commercial trainee" grated on my ears. It was just about the last form of vocational training I had hoped for. "Gracious me," said Fräulein Angerstein, who was still sitting there with a handful of stragglers, "anyone would think you were being sent to the scaffold, not out into the world!" My retort dismayed us both. "Maybe I am," I heard myself say, "or are you so sure I'm not?" She was somewhat startled, possibly by the realization of what form my future might take. "You can come and see me anytime," she told me—and I did.

As I made my way slowly out of the big school door through which I had so often raced with only seconds to spare before class, I offered up a silent prayer: "Not yet, please not yet . . ." My father was waiting outside No. 10, Mittelweg, just as he and my mother had waited ten years before with the bag of candies traditionally presented to German children on their first day in school. Despite everything, they had been good years. "Come on," my father said, "let's go and eat."

By this time, everyone was familiar with the "Jews Unwelcome" sign displayed by restaurants, inns, and cafés. Very few eating places had resisted the pressure to conform. One of them was the Vegetarisches Restaurant over the arcades beside the Kleine Alster, another a restaurant beside the elevated railroad station at Hoheluft Bridge. Signor Ferrari's Italian restaurant near the Alstertor also held out for a while. But when he was strongly urged, as a citizen of an Axis country, to put up one of the notices, he eventually did so. Although he allowed us to eat in a back room, our appetite for pasta was spoiled.

The day I left school we lunched at the Vegetarisches. All survivors of the Holocaust know what it is to dream, either of searching vainly for their murdered relatives, or of being reunited with them in pleasant times gone by. Whenever I dream of that lunch, the dream is a pleasant one.

One of our friends was a student of singing named Rainer Bujard. Young though he was, he had had his share of troubles. An "Aryan" with only one parent living, he was lucky enough to have his studies subsidized by Dr. Ascher, a respected Jewish physician who belonged to my parents' circle of acquaintances. Rainer had originally lived, more like a foster son than a lodger, with the doctor's daughter and her children. A few weeks prior to the evening on which he invited us to join him in celebrating my "going out into the world," he had been bullied into moving out by anti-Jewish neighbors who not only browbeat him but threatened his landlady and made the vilest insinuations against her. His new abode was a basement apartment, damp but romantic and inexpensive.

Little Inge had also been invited. "We must celebrate your coming of age!" Rainer insisted. I didn't find this "a consummation devoutly to be wished," but he knew the best way to console me. Seating himself at the piano, he raised his impressive bass voice in an aria from Verdi's *Falstaff*, which he was then studying.

Later we danced to the phonograph. One of the popular

hits of the day was a schmaltzy ballad in which the vocalist yearned to daydream with his or her beloved beneath the palm trees of Monte Carlo. My dearest wish that night would have been to loll beneath a palm tree, as far from Hamburg as possible.

Rainer was killed in the war.

After a year's experience of general office work, I was sick to death of sorting out files and keeping the petty cash. Herr Weber was an ultraconservative gentleman who never mentioned money (either you had it or you didn't), and my trainee's salary of fifteen marks a month—the going rate in those days—was hardly calculated to fire me with professional enthusiasm. This, allied to conditions at home, prompted me to terminate my traineeship.

In October 1938 I landed a so-called beginner's job with Herr Emil Todtmann of Beneckestrasse, a commercial representative dealing in "domestic and foreign alcoholic beverages." His office was in his apartment, and I fared extremely well there. Frau Todtmann, who loved making waffles, supplemented the rather inadequate diet I got at home by giving me hearty breakfasts. She and her husband were a humane, generous, and charitable couple. Herr Todtmann strove hard to overlook my failings in this uncongenial job. When he noticed how often I had trouble with my shorthand, for example, he allowed me to write in longhand. He had to let me go in the fall of 1939. The outbreak of war restricted the Germans to "domestic alcoholic beverages." They imported no more Veuve Clicquot (that was soon available to them in France, free of charge!), only the vermouths manufactured by Italy, their Axis partner, and those my former boss could handle on his own.

In 1954 Herr Todtmann wrote as follows to the Reparations Office: "When I interviewed Fräulein Hecht in 1938, she informed me that she had been obliged to abandon her traineeship after eighteen months in order to assist her parents financially. Her father's practice was steadily shrinking as a result of discriminatory legislation. . . . At the end of 1938 her father was sent to Oranienburg concentration camp and his practice was closed down. The family had a very bad time thereafter, which was why I so often came to their aid."

After the warmth of the atmosphere in Beneckestrasse, my next place of work left me cold. I briefly managed to survive in the Altona office of a construction executive, but only with the help of a cheerful Swedish colleague who taught me to say "Tack så mycket, jag mår bra" (Thanks a lot, I'm fine)—a phrase I often used on her. In January 1940 I became a clerk in a printing house on Hopfenmarkt, in the center of the Old City. The boss, Walter Prunst, put up with a great deal on my account, because summer 1940 was when my parents were arrested and sent to Fuhlsbüttel Prison via city hall, which became a notorious interrogation center. Eager to earn some extra money, I also worked evenings for a nearby chemical business. The managing director, Rolf Sommer, who very soon employed me full time, assisted victims of persecution in his own way. His partner, Dr. Pschorr, had a Jewish wife, and his attorney, Herbert Samuel, who had been articled to my father and became vice-president of Hamburg's municipal parliament after the war, was half-Jewish. Rolf Sommer courageously stood by them in defiance of his chief clerk, who was a Nazi.

I am still in touch with Elly R., who worked with me at this period. To quote from a letter she sent me when she heard

I was writing this book: "I still have a vivid recollection of the timid, dejected way your father came into the office. You urged him not to be scared of me, though, and told him I wasn't dangerous in spite of my swastika pin. I didn't understand at the time. Had I known what I know now, I'd have regarded it as a vile piece of Jew-baiting."

THE "NIGHT OF BROKEN GLASS" AND THE "LAMBETH WALK"

(1938)

11.10.38: Measures to Be Taken Against Jews To-night

Immediate preparations and consultations with police chiefs in attendance. Only those measures may be taken which carry no threat to German lives or property. (Synagogues to be burned only when there is no risk to the surrounding area.) No Jewish homes or business premises to be destroyed or looted; non-Jewish business premises to be protected; no Jews of foreign nationality to be molested. Summary confiscation by the police of documentary records belonging to Jewish religious communities. In all districts, as many Jews— well-to-do Jews in particular—are to be detained as can be accommodated in the detention centers available. Upon their request, the appropriate concentration camp must be contacted forthwith, so that they can be accommodated there as soon as possible. All State Police [Gestapo] headquarters are instructed not to intervene by taking countermeasures. (P. 253)

THE AUTHORITIES BEGAN to intensify our isolation in a deliberate, methodical way.

11.12.38:   *Jews are forbidden to frequent theaters, movie theaters, concerts, exhibitions, etc. (P. 255)*

That was outrageous enough, but it was very soon followed by a decree enjoining us to surrender our radio sets. With purposeful, insidious ingenuity, the persecuted were being cocooned in their own misery.

My father and I enjoyed going to the movies together, for instance to the Waterloo on Dammtorstrasse, where American films such as *San Francisco* or *Maytime* were premiered until 1939, or to the Urania, which showed cultural films. We no longer ventured into either theater after the above decree. A lawyer with an office on Jungfernstieg, however modest, might easily have been spotted.

One day our hankering for the "dream factory"—for ninety minutes' worth of something else to think about—became too much for us. (Young critics of old movies would find it easy to poke fun at our escapist dreams!) We headed for a poky little suburban movie house in Barmbek and asked for two good seats, because you could get a really stiff neck from sitting up front. All the good seats were taken, so we had to make the best of it. All of a sudden the usherette shone her flashlight over the first few rows and beckoned to us.

My heart stood still, my legs started trembling. Would we find ourselves confronted by two men in leather overcoats or brown or black uniforms? Had my father been recognized by someone?

"I have a box free now," the usherette said obligingly. She wasn't to know what she'd done. You couldn't have called us relieved—that would be far too mild a description—but going to the movies lost its appeal from then on.

Little Inge and I loved dancing. She was seventeen, I only sixteen, and in those days, when the age of majority was twenty-one, we had to get our parents' permission first. My mother rarely consented to chaperone us to a tea dance. Aside from the fact that we had no money to spare for tickets or dance dresses, she had other worries.

"Then for heaven's sake let us go on our own," we pleaded. "After all, we have to act grown-up enough in other respects." We enlisted the support of our fathers, who sadly backed us up. They appreciated how very far from carefree we were for our age. Carefree? By now, no dancing school, tennis club, or athletics club would accept us.

So we proudly set off, that summer afternoon in 1938, for the Orchideenkaffee near Dammtor station, once the site of a small zoo that my father and I had often visited on our Sunday walks together. I had saved up to buy myself a dark blue blouse of watered taffeta—the latest thing. It went against the grain to wear it with the skirt of my gray working suit, but I couldn't afford anything more suitable. The sun shone, the dance floor gleamed, and Laszlo Kurucz and his band struck us as "terrific."

When our rhythmical cavortings were interrupted by a Haydn minuet, we were joined at our table by my partner, Hans T. Little Inge and I had developed the knack of conjuring magical experiences out of very modest pleasures. To most people this would have been a run-of-the-mill tea dance—an experience to be repeated whenever they felt inclined; to us it was a whole succession of magical moments. That evening I called my parents and asked permission to stay out a bit longer. Hans was not only grown-up but "very respectable," I assured them, and he wanted to take me to "Tante Clara's." This was a popular cellar bar owned by a wine merchant named Benthin, whose plump and cheerful wife, Tante Clara, supplied the musical entertainment. Seated on stools around the upturned barrels that served as tables, customers listened raptly as she leveled a long pointer at a sheet of painted canvas and celebrated the funny pictures on it in song, accompanied by an accordion. Everyone joined in the choruses. Above us, swaying in a blue haze of tobacco smoke from countless pipes, dangled dried or imitation fish and carved wooden ships of all shapes and sizes. To the sixteen-year-old from Harvestehude, it was a unique and unforgettable occasion.

Hans, who was exactly twice my age, delivered a carefully worded speech while walking me home: a man of his mature years could very quickly tell whether two people were compatible, he was old enough to marry and keen to do so, and we must definitely get to know each other better.

I felt like Cinderella when the clock struck twelve. "I'm a leper," I told him. He thought I was drunk until I explained what a "first degree half-breed" was.

Principiis obsta! We resolved not to see each other again. It was a bad moment—my worst to date.

Then, one afternoon while I was still working for the patent attorney, Hans called me at the office. "I had a business appointment with the Gestapo at city hall," he said. He was an interior designer. "I inquired about our chances of obtaining a marriage permit. It can be done, you told me so yourself." I was almost speechless. "For God's sake," I said, "only on paper. Don't go giving those madmen ideas, or they'll watch us like hawks." Hans was unimpressed. "Not them," he said. "Friendly dissuasion, that's all they gave me." But I persisted. "It's impossible," I told him. "You'd risk losing your municipal contracts." The municipal contracts were a family tradition that dated back to his father's time.

Hans risked a lot more than that. One day, almost a year after our first and hitherto only meeting, we bumped into each other on the street. "There's no such thing as coincidence," he said, "only fate." And he bore me off to a dance hall on the corner of Lehmweg and Eppendorfer Weg. There was a little red light over the door. Innocuous though the place was, my parents wouldn't have approved—not that it took much to arouse parental misgivings in those days. Its name was the Half Moon.

We didn't talk about ourselves, just danced. Hans walked me home with a moon—a real one—hovering overhead. "We'll stick together," he said, "sink or swim." I was seventeen. Our daughter Barbara was born two and a half years later, by which time Hans was in the army.

In June 1938 Little Inge and I were christened by Pastor Walter Schmidt of Bremen, the husband of my mother's closest girlhood friend—a precautionary step of which he thoroughly approved. At least on paper—and at first glance—we no longer floated in a dangerous, conspicuous vacuum, though our baptismal certificates naturally made no difference to the "reprehensible" mixture of blood that flowed in our veins.

In November 1938 I traveled to Berlin to stay with my friend Manon and the new man in her life, a photographer named Umbo. I also saw my Aunt Alice, who was working as a nurse in a Jewish old people's home. She had invited me to dine with her at a restaurant on the night of November 10, because conditions at the home were deplorable, and I found the place so unutterably depressing that I wouldn't have eaten a bite. Once well-to-do but now stripped of their possessions and evicted from their houses and apartments, the poor old inmates waited with almost apathetic resignation—for what, they had no clear idea. . . .

There was a sudden commotion in the restaurant entrance, and some uniformed Nazis came tramping into the hushed, peaceful dining room. Their appearance instantly and irrevocably transformed our outlook on life. It was my very first sight of evil in action. The "non-Aryan" diners were hustled outside, so shocked and startled that none of them uttered a sound. Nothing could be heard but their receding footsteps, and I saw only one woman burst into tears.

My aunt remained quite calm. One of the uniformed figures marched up to our table. "I'm crippled in one leg, and my Christian niece accompanied me here." The only response was a barked request: "Papers!" With trembling fingers, I groped in my purse for my identity card. "So you aren't a Jewess?" I swallowed hard. "I live with my mother—she's the Aryan half of a privileged mixed marriage." How fluently the idiotic Nazi jargon came tripping off my tongue! The Brownshirt turned to my aunt. "And you're a nurse in an old folks' home?" Our papers were returned and the invaders left.

"I probably owe you my freedom," said Aunt Alice, "—for now." The truck that had been parked outside drove off at once. I couldn't face any more food, but Aunt Alice, ever practical, urged me to eat up. "You mustn't lose your appetite over a thing like that," she said. "This is only the start."

Too overwrought to sleep, Manon and I talked the rest of the night away. Being a half-Jewish divorcée, Manon couldn't legally marry her "Aryan" boyfriend, but she planned to go through a form of marriage on some little Baltic island where it mightn't occur to the local mayor to ask for her "Aryan credentials." She didn't succeed, incidentally, unlike another friend of mine, Ingrid L. Although such marriages were invalid, the neighbors weren't to know, so they regarded Ingrid's little son Kai as legitimate—a more important consideration then than it is now. The baby's stalwart "Aryan" father, a well-paid whaler, was away at sea and thus out of sight of the guardians of the law. They forgot him until war broke out, but he was later killed in action.

I caught a train back to Hamburg the next morning. The hours that preceded my departure were destined to go down in history as Kristallnacht, the "Night of Broken Glass." Just how "spontaneous" this eruption of "popular fury" was—the Nazis used these expressions ad nauseam—can be gauged from the phenomenal speed with which the following decrees were issued:

11.12.38: Executive Order Pertaining to the Restoration of the Appearance of Streets in Respect of Jewish Business Premises

1. All damage sustained by Jewish business premises and

homes in consequence of public indignation at interna-
tional Jewry's campaign against National Socialist Ger-
many will at once be made good by Jewish householders
and tradespeople.

2. The cost of repairs will be borne by the owners of the
Jewish businesses and residences affected. All insurance
claims lodged by Jews of German nationality will be
sequestered for the benefit of the State. (P. 254)

On November 9, the third secretary of the German embassy in Paris, Ernst Eduard vom Rath, had been assassinated by a German Jewish refugee named Herschel Grynspan. Strangely enough, our authorities must have had prior knowledge of this incident.

This murder heralded the darkest period in our country's history, becoming a justification for all that ensued—all that might have been foreseen by any reader of Hitler's *Mein Kampf*: it ultimately led to the Final Solution.

Every decree issued between then and 1945 was one more nail in the coffin of human dignity and human life itself. To quote Robert Kempner's introduction to *Das Sonderrecht für die Juden im NS-Staat*:

"They were deprived of their occupations, robbed of their property, forbidden to inherit or bequeath, forbidden to sit on park benches or keep canaries, forbidden to use public transportation [Author's note: except to a very limited degree], forbidden to frequent restaurants, concerts, theaters, and movie houses. They were subject to specific racial laws, stripped of all their civil rights, denied freedom of movement. Their human rights and human dignity were trampled in the dust until they were deported to concentration camps and consigned to the gas chambers."

This process, with all its atrocious concomitants, began on November 10, 1938.

11.10.38:   *Further to tonight's directive from CdSiPo [chief of Se-curity Police], I advise you that Dachau, Buchenwald, and Sachsenhausen [Oranienburg] concentration camps are each in a position to accommodate ten thousand de-tainees. (P. 253)*

11.10.38:   *Jews found with arms in their possession are to be held in custody for twenty years. (P. 253)*

November 11 was my brother's birthday. We had laid the table and lit fifteen candles, but we waited in vain for my father to turn up. He had been ordered off a streetcar and taken to Oranienburg-Sachsenhausen concentration camp, near Berlin.

I recorded my impressions of his homecoming in December 1938. The magazine *Umschau* published them in 1947—my very first appearance in print. Everything was still so fresh in my mind that I found it hard to take a detached view of what had happened.

One day we received a card with a red border. "Sender: Detainee Felix Hecht. Detainee's No. . . ." Then: "Oranien-burg Concentration Camp, near Berlin." He was released shortly before Christmas.

12.12.38:   *All Jewish detainees over the age of fifty are to be released. Discharged prisoners must report to the police at once. (P. 266)*

He turned up with a shaven skull, bent and gaunt, a weary man with weary eyes. And he was so cold, so very cold. The cold had stored itself in his limbs while he was breaking stones in the teeth of the icy November wind. Camp regulations prescribed light clothing only, and anyone who secreted newspaper under his shirt for warmth was beaten half to death. It had been intimated to my father and all the others released that day in December 1938 that anyone who spoke of his detention outside would be in serious trouble. We *wanted* him to speak, though. Our discretion went without saying, and anyway, he had to tell someone. In a low voice punctuated by the hollow cough that lingered with him for a long time to come, he recounted his terrible experiences. If he hadn't been our own father, a qualified lawyer, and in his right mind, we would never have believed him.

But we had to resume our daily lives and be our normal selves without even hinting at what we had heard. The Todtmanns were the only people I dared confide in. Frau Todtmann gave me a big package of groceries for my father and told me, with absolute sincerity, "The Führer knows nothing of this."

We "half-breeds" were slowly becoming inured to fear. "Aryan" friends would sometimes invite us to share their relatively carefree existence. We were fortunate in having these opportunities to enjoy ourselves in cheerful company, unlike our Jewish friends and relations, but we also had to live with the awareness of being better off than they were. The real sufferers didn't begrudge us our fun, but we weren't always as generous to ourselves.

During the summer of 1938, a London dance craze had crossed the channel and caught on at the Café Vaterland, where patrons were taught the steps at teatime on the little circular dance floor. The "Lambeth Walk" was an innocently amusing novelty dance with a catchy tune. One afternoon Hans and I whiled away an hour or two prancing around and clapping our hands obediently in time to the music.

Then came the inevitable letdown. "Who knows," I said as we were walking home, "that may be one of our pleasantest memories ever." It was a prescient remark.

Being English, the "Lambeth Walk" was of course banned when war broke out. When I first heard it again in 1980, the memories it revived were bittersweet.

THE FIRST YEAR
OF THE WAR
(1939)

10.17.39: *If Jews and persons of German blood occupy the same building, and if the Germans* [sic!] *constitute the majority of the occupants of that building, the Jews will not take part in air raid practices. If the contrary applies, Jews will carry out practices on their own. (P. 306)*

PRIOR TO THE INTRODUCTION of the yellow star which every Jew had to wear, someone had come up with another bright idea:

8.17.38:   *From 1.1.39 Jews who do not bear one of the forenames listed as a Jewish forename in the Interior Ministry circular dated 8.18.38 must assume the name "Israel" (for male persons) or "Sara" (for female persons). (P. 237)*

Because my father's first name was Felix—the Happy One!— and not Isaak, Isidor, or Mosche, he, too, received a new birth certificate from Registry Office 3a, Kolonnaden 3, Hamburg. It bore the following note: "The aforesaid child has assumed the additional name 'Israel.' "

It was as simple as that. From now on, anyone who asked to see your identity card could tell your racial origins at a glance. By the time passports were stamped with a "J," as they very soon were, no person of the Jewish faith could travel abroad unrecognized for what he was.

On January 28, 1939, my father received a letter from the Gestapo revoking his permission to appear before the Hamburg courts.

9.27.38: Executive Order Pertaining to the Reich Citizenship Law

> *The profession of attorney is closed to Jews. Any Jews still practicing as attorneys will quit the bar by 11.30.38 (or, in certain cases, somewhat later). The judicatory will permit Jewish legal consultants to advise and represent Jews. Veterans among the retiring attorneys may, if in need, be granted revocable subsistence allowances payable out of the incomes of Jewish legal consultants. The latter will retain a proportion of their fees as remuneration. (P. 242)*

There being no well-to-do Jewish clients left, my father's income had dried up. He was therefore entitled to claim a subsistence allowance under the 1938 decree, though this was a laborious and demeaning business. I came across a letter from the Bar Association in Berlin, dated November 1941, which allotted my father RM 170 a month but warned him to expect further cuts in the future. It additionally pointed out that he qualified for a grant only because he had two underage children.

Like many communications from attorneys who had taken over the clients and, thus, the incomes of their Jewish colleagues, this letter conveyed not a shadow of regret, not a hint of shame. Its tone was chilly.

My wages as an office worker just about covered our monthly gas bill, once I had deducted an agreed share for myself, so we drew a supplementary allowance from the public welfare office—not in those days a legal entitlement. In return for this meager financial support, lucky though we were to get it at all, my mother had to work in a frightful sewing room a long way from home. She also earned some extra money by cleaning house for a doctor's wife in the neighborhood. This lady, who was a Tartar in other respects, overlooked her lack of dexterity with a bucket and scrubbing brush and her inability to polish tiles and parquet floors. At least she was one of those who secretly deplored our lot.

One evening our lodger Ali took me to Schwanenwiek to see a friend named Hans Wolffheim, whom we found ensconced amid piles of books in a little garret overlooking the Alster.

Ali introduced us. "Aside from being as much of a mongrel as you are," he told me, "Hans has more brains than anyone I know." He turned to Wolffheim. "Tell her your specialties, Hans."

Wolffheim, who was another "first degree half-breed," shrugged and smiled. "Philosophy, German, English—oh yes, and psychology, worse luck."

"And now," said Ali, "he sits here vegetating."

"Surely not," I said, surveying all the books. Hans Wolffheim had taken a degree in 1933, just in time, but the Nuremberg Laws disqualified him from joining the university faculty. Restricted to "employment of a subordinate nature," he spent his days working in a textile factory. It was 1946 before he obtained a lectureship, though he was subsequently appointed to the chair of modern German literature at Hamburg.

Wolffheim derived a certain pleasure from my interest in literature. He used to read aloud to us for hours on end, notably from such authors as Thomas Mann, in exile since 1933, and Karl Wolfskehl, who had lived in Italy until 1938 and fled from the Fascists to New Zealand. (Wolffheim later founded a study center for expatriate German literature at Hamburg

University.) A friend of ours from now on, he occasionally rustled up some genuine Indian tea, which was getting steadily scarcer. To me, tea was not only conversationally stimulating but something akin to an elixir of life.

For victims of Nazi oppression, the outbreak of war on September 1, 1939, spelled emotional conflicts of unimaginable intensity. Nazi Germany's enemies were, after all, our potential liberators. Every bomb that fell brought liberation nearer, but it also fell on us, our friends and neighbors—on the people to whom we had belonged till 1933.

In 1946, when I called on the chief rabbi of the Jewish community in Freiburg, who had recently returned from Theresienstadt, in the hope of learning something about my father's fate, he asked when I had last been in Hamburg. "Not since the terror raids of July 1943," I told him. Goebbels's term for Allied air attacks came quite naturally to me—it had passed into our vocabulary, too—but the old man nearly exploded. In his view, no response to German acts of aggression could be termed a "terror raid."

> 9.1.39: *By order of local police authorities, Jews are prohibited from walking the streets (being outside their homes) after 8 P.M. (9 P.M. in summer). (P. 303)*

Even my "privileged" father had to observe this rule as far as possible. We had long ago ceased to speculate on the reasons for such edicts. Foreigners must have found them less intelligible, however, because on September 15, 1939, a "confidential directive" was issued to the German press:

> 9.15.39 *Foreign newspapers have stated that Jews in Germany are no longer permitted to walk the streets after 8 P.M. This*

is correct. All local authorities in the Reich have issued an order to that effect, on the ground that Jews have not infrequently taken advantage of the blackout to molest Aryan women. (P. 305)

9.20.39:   *Jews of German nationality and stateless Jews are forbidden to own radio receivers. This prohibition covers Aryans living on Jewish premises, and also half-breeds. Special regulations apply to mixed marriages. (P. 305)*

Because we lived with our "Aryan" mother, we could turn on the radio as often as we liked. Whenever we listened to music, to a concert or a lecture, it heightened our sense of guilt at being better off than our neighbors.

"RACIAL DISGRACE"
AND PLANS TO EMIGRATE
(1940)

9.18.35:   *Persons implicated in cases of racial disgrace are to be taken into custody. (P. 131)*

9.26.35:   *Where instances of "racially disgraceful conduct" antedate the promulgation of the new Jewish laws, authorities are recommended to refrain from drastic measures except in particularly flagrant cases of seduction or rape.*

   Those committing offenses subsequent to the promulgation of the new Jewish laws will be ruthlessly prosecuted. (P. 132)

WHEN WILL IT BE our turn? The thought that had haunted our lives like a waking nightmare became reality, as it had for so many others, a few weeks before Easter 1940. Here is how I described it to the Hamburg Reparations Office in September 1961, in support of a (rejected) claim for compensation:

"Some weeks before Easter, my mother was arrested for allegedly committing an act of 'racial disgrace' with her divorced husband, my father, and taken to city hall. My father, who had lived with us for five years after the divorce and paid us regular visits thereafter, was also arrested.

"Late the same evening, my mother came home. She fainted on entering the apartment, and we put her to bed. When she recovered consciousness, she enlisted the advice of our lodger Ali. Apparently, she had been threatened and bullied, under extremely undignified circumstances, into admitting an act of 'racial disgrace.' She now wished to retract this admission at once, in writing. An attorney, Dr. Harms, called on us and took her retraction down. The Gestapo's response was to summon my mother again by telephone, though she was really in no fit state to leave her bed. 'Detainee Sillich'—as she had to call herself when reporting her presence, standing at attention in her cell—was not reunited with us until the Thursday before Easter, three weeks later. My father was released the same day. I myself paid one visit to city hall through the good offices of Dr. Harms. Though treated in an exceedingly sarcastic manner, I was informed that I could deliver some articles of clothing to the Hamburg-Fuhlsbüttel detention center. After her release, my mother told us that she had had to sign a written undertaking never to see my father again, and that she was to be held responsible for ensuring that my brother and I formed no relationships with 'Aryan' partners. Otherwise, she would at once be rearrested.

"We do not know whether such statements were to be taken seriously. What is certain is that from then until April 23, 1945, the date of our liberation in Staufen/Breisgau, my mother never shook off her terrible fears and has since required constant medical attention."

This factual account cannot convey our state of mind during those weeks. But for our friend Ali and the attorney, who made unremitting efforts to secure our parents' release, the suspense would have been almost unbearable, because no word of their fate was allowed to filter through to us.

I began by describing the world in which my mother grew up. During her three weeks in custody—over which I prefer to draw a veil—she began to feel as if her childhood were only a dream. The two worlds seemed so utterly incompatible.

"That first day," she said, "I met the kind of girls I'd never come up against before. . . ."

"Whores, you mean?"

She was relieved that I'd absolved her from saying the word. It had never passed her lips before, any more than the girls themselves had formed part of her social environment.

"They were old hands, you see. They couldn't have been

nicer—they teased me a little for being so frightened and impractical, but they weren't in there for political reasons and had no conception of what it meant. They rolled me some cigarettes—out of butts, imagine!" We couldn't repress a wry laugh at this, but she went on, "You'd never believe how quickly a person can grow to appreciate anything that seems like a humane gesture in inhumane surroundings. . . ."

But what had actually led up to her imprisonment?

April 1942: *Jews are forbidden to visit the homes of Aryans and persons living in mixed matrimony. (P. 369)*

This regulation was observed long before it appeared in writing, but who would have dreamed that the Nuremberg Laws could apply to a divorced couple who had produced two "offspring"? Well, now we knew.

The layout of our Hansastrasse apartment proved disastrous. Originally one floor of a spacious town house, it had later been divided into two suites of rooms separated by a communicating door, which could be locked. Anyone wanting to pay us a visit in the rear suite had to pass through the suite at the front. The latter was rented by a small, private old people's home, and it was those ladies, Party members one and all, who had denounced my parents.

We continued to live cheek by jowl with them—we had no choice—but my father had to shun their "Aryan" orbit from then on, and was consequently banished from the family table.

The former Fräulein von Sillich, who had once been privileged to receive a letter of condolence from the duke of Meiningen on the sudden death of her father (she reverently preserved it in a casket) and had seen that same father buried with full military honors—whose upbringing, in short, had been founded on the traditional values of the imperial era—had now become acquainted with certain previously unimagined and unimaginable things: for example, the inside of a jail. Much the same could be said of Felix Hecht, erstwhile sergeant of the Seventh (Seydlitz) Cuirassiers, a regiment of heavy cavalry based at Halberstadt. For all his experience of life and knowledge of the world, he had found it impossible to conceive—until *Kristallnacht*—that his active service in the First World War, which earned him the Iron Cross Second Class (Jewish soldiers were seldom awarded any higher decoration), would fail to protect him from the gathering storm.

One day in the summer of 1940 I was summoned to report for a medical examination. All German girls not undergoing higher education or vocational training were obliged to do a year's national service, usually as farmhands or domestic help for mothers of large families. "Oh God," I groaned to Hans Wolffheim, "that's all I needed!" After the treatment we'd received from them, did the authorities really expect us to perform this "honorary service" for the German nation?

Wolffheim came around the same evening, bearing a packet of tea. "Drink some just before your medical," he advised, faintly amused at the idea of a townee like me wielding a pick and shovel. "We're so unused to the stuff these days, it's bound to give you palpitations."

So I drank plenty—I've seldom enjoyed the delicious beverage less—and reported to the medical center. It was crowded with "Aryan" girls. Most of them seemed in high spirits, and anyone who may secretly have been unenthusiastic took care not to show it. The doctor treated me sympathetically, in a detached sort of way, because I saw no reason to conceal my "half-breed" status and circumstances. Although he might have

74

drafted me on principle, he didn't. He returned my employment record stamped "Compulsory One-Year Service Deferred." My deferment ran for only twelve months, but by 1941 the authorities had largely stopped bothering about the likes of us.

Incidental note: I needn't have drunk all that tea—I'd have had palpitations anyway.

[1935:]   Re Art and Antique Dealers

> *Pursuant to paragraph 10 of Decree No. 1 pertaining to the implementation of the Reich Chamber of Culture Law of 11.1.33, I refuse you admission to the Reich Chamber of Fine Arts and debar you from continuing to pursue the occupation of art and antique dealer. I grant you four weeks' grace in which to reorganize or liquidate your business.* (P. 149)

Uncle Edgar, who had taken over the Rembrandthaus, my grandfather's old and reputable business in the Colonnades, was also affected by a decree of this nature. Although trade had dwindled badly, we were much attached to the remains of this onetime family institution. Now it was to be "reorganized," in this case meaning sold. The purchaser, I believe, was the firm's former janitor.

Most of my father's fellow attorneys had emigrated, and his only partner had committed suicide. How could he emigrate, though, without a vestige of capital, without us children, and, last but not least, with no hope of reestablishing his practice in some foreign land? He was too old to go to Palestine as a pioneer. Doctors could make a fresh start abroad without too much difficulty, whereas lawyers had no such professional prospects. Honduras and Shanghai were potential places of

75

refuge for impecunious Jews, though certain restrictions applied there, too.

"What on earth could I do in a Chinese city?" my father protested, and he had a point. What *could* a Hamburg attorney have done in the Far East, in a city that had been occupied by Japan, an Axis power, since its seizure from the Chinese in 1937?

My relatives from Hagedornstrasse, Uncle Edgar, Aunt Hanna, and cousin Hans, booked passage to Shanghai in 1940. They offered to send written confirmation, on arrival, that they would house me if I chose to join them there. I could then get some kind of job and try to arrange a passage for my father as well.

I agreed, though without any clear idea of what I was doing. Perhaps I saw it as my father's last chance of escape, but what of my unfortunate mother? She had already lost her health and her faith in human nature. Was she now to lose her family into the bargain?

"You'll still have Wolfgang," I consoled her, "and we'll probably be able to come back sometime."

For the present, however, Hitler's armies remained victorious.

It all went very quickly. Jews were confined to their homes after dark and the train didn't leave the central station until midnight, so it was late afternoon when the Hechts made their way to the Hotel Reichshof to while away their last night in Germany. Because of the curfew, only Little Inge and I could accompany them.

The emigrants were depressed, dispirited, and filled with premature homesickness. Our family had, after all, lived on the banks of the Elbe for two generations. Besides, we all dreaded that some terrible hitch might occur at the last moment, because it went without saying that the permits and papers had to be examined yet again by some official of forbidding mien. All in all, it was a lugubrious occasion.

When the time came, we escorted the trio across the darkened street to the gloomy station entrance. "Please don't come onto the platform with us," said Aunt Hanna, then: "Happy landings in Shanghai!" (When they got there, any exultation the new arrivals felt was dampened by the sight of a swastika flag flying from the masthead of a German ship berthed alongside the Huangpu waterfront!)

In February 1982 I was reminded of my Aunt Hanna's descriptions of life in Shanghai by a West German radio reconstruction of this largely unknown form of emigration.

The Oriental mentality forbade "whites," or Europeans in general, to perform "menial" tasks. German Jews elsewhere in the world had long ago abandoned such class-conscious notions, many of them having gone into domestic service in Britain and the United States. In Shanghai, however, European and American residents impressed on all newcomers that these unwritten rules must be observed. A local Jewish Welfare Association saw to it that emigrants were housed and communally fed, but they found their enforced idleness hard to bear. Only the craftsmen among them, most of whom came from Eastern Europe, managed to set up small workshops and escape from the slums. This came to a stop in May 1943, when all stateless persons, including Jewish immigrants, were herded together and confined in a ghetto. The craftsmen, too, were forced to abandon the fruits of their hard work and move to the ghetto, a slum quarter infested with typhus and cholera. Many of the inmates died.

I was naturally unaware of this when the promised letter arrived and I began making arrangements to leave for Shanghai. While my poor mother suffered in courageous silence (as befitted an officer's daughter) and my father bottled up his sense of guilt, I myself succumbed to a thrill of anticipation and adventure. After all, I was still technically a child.

Our last objets d'art were sold, and the balance of my fare was given me by a friend of the family, the writer William Quindt, who lived in Blankenese. A well-traveled man with a wide knowledge of people and places at home and abroad—he had been press agent for the Sarrasani Circus for years—Herr Quindt not only detested the Nazis to the point of nausea but helped us on numerous occasions. I presented my papers, obtained a travel permit, and bought my Trans-Siberian Railroad ticket. To a twenty-year-old in the days when foreign travel was neither as commonplace nor as relatively inexpensive as it is today, nothing could have seemed more glamorously exotic, especially in wartime.

I felt quite odd when my fingers finally closed on the sheaf of tickets that would take me all the way across the Soviet Union to China. When the odd sensation persisted and I started feeling actively sick, I went to the doctor. "You're going to have a baby," he told me.

I handed back my tickets and wrote to Shanghai. My dear, good mother now had occasion to discover that even an illegitimate grandchild—a phenomenon alien to her world of ideas—deserved to be hailed with joy if it banished her misgivings about a daughter's departure for the Far East.

And my father's prospects of emigrating? "Never mind," he said, "I'm delighted about the baby." For a while he was alone in his delight. I was filled with foreboding.

My cousin Jack Hecht, now a resident of Alamo, California, tape-recorded his recollections for me in September 1982:

"We left Hamburg in 1940, when I was eight years old. From Hamburg we traveled by train via Berlin to Danzig, then on by air to Moscow, where we boarded the Trans-Siberian Express. We traveled across the USSR for a whole week, through Siberia to Vladivostok, then to Harbin in Manchukuo and on to Dairen. It was awfully cold, I remember, and I couldn't understand why we had to go so far from home. From Dairen we sailed down the Chinese coast in a little steamer, sleeping in the hold with some Japanese soldiers. We reached Shanghai two days later.

"We were greeted by the Jewish community, and my father managed to rent us a room—we referred to it as a small apartment—in the French concession. In those days Shanghai was an international settlement under Japanese control and British, French, and American supervision. In our quarter the street names were French, as were the police and the military. My father, who had three hundred dollars on deposit at a Japanese bank, used the money to open a small art dealer's shop. The local inhabitants were very interested in objets d'art. We had divided up the premises, and we ate and slept there, too. The foreign troops withdrew when war broke out between Japan and America after the attack on Pearl Harbor, and the Japanese occupied the entire city without firing a shot. That was in December 1941.

"In May 1943 the Japanese decreed that all stateless persons not in possession of passports should move to Hongkiu, a ghetto area. This decree principally affected the Jewish immigrants, who now, like my father, lost their modest livelihoods all over again. Father was assigned one room, and we had to share the kitchen and bathroom with six other families.

No interest in art could survive under such circumstances, and our minor material advantages came to an end.

"I went to the Jewish community school, where German teachers taught us the usual subjects. We boys played football and the grown-ups founded sports clubs, so life went on like that all through the war. American bombers sometimes raided Japanese military installations in the city.

"Then came July 17, 1945. It was a very cloudy day. I and a lot of other children were playing outside the house where we lived. We could hear airplanes but not see them, the clouds were so thick. They came nearer, and when I looked up at the sky I saw little black specks of dust raining down on us. They were bombs. One of them exploded in front of our house. I ran into the kitchen. The entrance was behind the house. Everything was littered with glass, and the plaster was flaking off the walls. My father came toward me, bleeding from a big wound over his heart. He was still on his feet. I shouted, 'Papa, you're wounded!' Then he collapsed. A piece of shrapnel must have sailed through the open window and hit him. My mother was unhurt. She'd been in the kitchen, my father in the living room.

"I still believe that something could have been done for my father if so many people around us hadn't been injured at the same time. He bled to death. The doctors couldn't be everywhere at once.

"The war ended in August 1945, and the Jewish community of America sent us money, food, and clothing. There were eighteen thousand of us by that time, all immigrants from Germany, Austria, Poland, and Hungary."

That was how my nice, jovial Uncle Edgar met his end. Although Aunt Hanna never got over his death, she was a very courageous woman. She trained to become a nurse and worked at a Shanghai hospital until she and cousin Hans were offered a chance to emigrate to San Francisco in the summer of 1949.

I've often wondered where *I* would have been during that air raid, in the kitchen or the living room. . . .

I tried to find out how the Jews of Shanghai were treated by the Nazi Party's local representatives. A diplomat who was stationed there at the time told me that the Japanese didn't give "a damn" about the Nazis' anti-Jewish campaign. They simply confined all stateless persons in Hongkiu.

The Japanese who acted as "boss" of the ghetto, a man named Goya, was interned by the Americans. According to cousin Hans, they later released him because he had refused to do what the Nazis allegedly asked him to do: build some gas chambers.

THE LONG YEAR
(1941)

9.1.41: *With effect from 9.15.41, Jews who have attained the age of seven are forbidden to show themselves in public without a Jewish star. Jews are forbidden to leave their residential area without written police permission, and to wear decorations or other medals.*

This does not apply to Jewish husbands living in mixed matrimony if there exist offspring of their marriages who do not count as Jews, or if their only son has been killed in action, nor to Jewish wives of childless mixed marriages for the duration of such marriages. (P. 347)

As soon as I knew I was pregnant, I wrote to Hans. Although it was a hazardous and impractical course of action, he spoke to his sergeant, the first person in authority to approach when applying for permission to marry (which was sometimes granted, so it was said, though never to my knowledge). The outcome was disastrous, of course. When Barbara was born he wrote me from the Russian front that he hoped he would never come back. That wasn't a very cheering letter for a young mother to receive during her confinement, but I'd grown accustomed to expecting nothing, not even consolation. Hans had gone through a great deal by that time, partly on my account and partly because of his appalling experiences at the front.

His wish was fulfilled. He paid one visit to Hamburg and made his little daughter's acquaintance, but was killed in action at Lepel on June 29, 1944.

I needed a maternity dress and was allocated some extra clothing coupons. My mother and I set off on a shopping expedition. While we were walking down Grindelallee, something unforgettable happened.

Father was coming toward us on the other side of the street. We caught sight of each other at the same instant. Mother turned deathly pale and stopped short. Father, too, paused for a moment. "For God's sake keep moving," I said. "Someone may be spying on us—they may think we arranged it." Mother walked on. Father walked on. Mother started crying.

"Shall we buy the silly dress another time?" I asked.

"No," she said, "that wouldn't help either." Then she said, "If I'd known all this, I'd never have divorced him. If anything happens to him, I'll always feel I'm to blame."

She nursed that belief till the day she died in 1979. It was a long time.

My father had been compelled to move out when the Edgar Hechts left for Shanghai. He now lived in one small room in Dillstrasse, which had gradually become a kind of ghetto. That room, with its bed, bookcase, hot plate, and cluttered chairs, still haunts my dreams. . . .

My father liked to keep a miniature reference library of newspaper articles on subjects of particular interest to him. That had presented few problems in a house or apartment, but in one diminutive room? He needed an occupation that would take his mind off things, now more than ever, so the walls were lined with ever-growing mountains of newsprint.

Did we devote enough attention to him at this time? Why didn't we go and help him sort out his stacks of newspapers? Why didn't we cook for him? I still have his cookbook, the flyleaf of which bears a note of the pages to be consulted when braising steak and cooking rice. He was fifty-seven years old and a stranger to the inside of a kitchen when he started experimenting with a hot plate.

Why trouble to record such details? Because they form

part of the mosaic. One's conscience can be pricked by the strangest little things. . . .

My father was exempted from wearing a star. So, of course, was my mother, and the same applied to Wolfgang and me. Little Inge's position was different because her mother had converted to Judaism on her marriage, so the children of that marriage were *Geltungsjuden*, a Nazi neologism implying that they were technically and formally Jewish. By a very rare stroke of good fortune, Little Inge's status remained temporarily undetected. Besides, we had both been baptized in 1938. Although this wouldn't have helped in a real emergency, there were occasions when officials refrained from insisting on documentary proof of one's "Aryan" ancestry. Little Inge's father did have to wear the star, however, because he had divorced her mother at her own request and married a Jewess.

Our relations and many of our friends were obliged to wear what the Nazis regarded as a badge of shame, which had by law to be prominently displayed. When "star wearers" paid us a visit, they would try to obscure or conceal the yellow emblem because all such visits were prohibited. We had good reason to fear the Nazi crones in the front apartment, but we also feared for ourselves. We feared that someday, if an explosive situation arose, we ourselves would avert our eyes, say nothing, walk on—that we ourselves would be found wanting in what was termed backbone.

3.29.41: *The Reich Association [of Jews] has until April 1, 1941, to supply the RSHA [Central State Security Bureau] with a full list of all Jewish apartments in Aryan buildings. This list must include addresses, number of rooms, and additional details. (P. 338)*

There was an acceleration and accumulation of horrors in 1941. The first trainloads of deportees left for the East, and decrees were issued with the ultimate aim of "expelling" the Jews. These ranged from the registration of their living quarters and all their possessions to the following, logical, edict:

11.15.42: *Jews may no longer keep household pets. (P. 364)*

I say logical, because the authors of the Final Solution wished to spare themselves the necessity of slaughtering abandoned pets as well as their owners.

Jews were also subject to increasingly ominous cuts in their food rations. Unless they received covert help—and many tradespeople were secretly charitable to their long-established Jewish customers—they wasted away for all to see (not that their plight hadn't been universally obvious ever since the wearing of yellow stars was made compulsory).

Then came another turn of the screw:

4.20.41: *Foodstuffs received by Jews in packages from abroad are to be deducted from their food rations. (P. 339)*

All else apart, Jews had been treated as enemies since the outbreak of war, and their German nationality had been revoked.

For all that, "first degree half-breeds" like us had many aids to distraction, notably the movies. When I saw a 1982 revival of *Quax der Bruchpilot*, a Heinz Rühmann comedy made in 1941, my mind went back to the wartime evening when Little Inge and I had reveled in its innocent humor. Rühmann had poked fun at the concept of iron discipline with admirable

88

understatement, though without actually demolishing it. Germany was fighting a war, after all, even if it wasn't his war or ours. (We only found out later that he was one of the many stars whose marriages to or relationships with "non-Aryans" put them at Goebbels's mercy, so they couldn't have been half as cheerful as they had to make out!) Thank you anyway, Heinz Rühmann, for giving us so much enjoyment.

Not wanting the evening to end as soon as the movie was over, we headed for a little wine bar in Grindelallee, close enough to home for us to get back in time if the air raid sirens sounded an early warning. Almost at once, we were joined at our table by two SS men. Little Inge, whose blonde hair was almost certainly to blame for this dubious honor, made a warning noise in her throat. "Aryan" girls could have afforded to get up and go; we couldn't.

Our companions were caricatures of their kind: glass eyes would have looked more human. I am adding nothing and leaving a good deal unsaid when I record that, during our conversation, one of them suddenly began to brag about his maltreatment of Jews in a concentration camp. Although many SS men would never have dreamed of raising the subject, I'm sure, this one really did. I don't recall how we managed to get away, but we never again visited the place unescorted.

We were sitting at the breakfast table on June 22, 1941, when Ali came rushing in. Pale to the roots of his hair, he told us that Hitler had declared war on Russia.

Ali once took me and Little Inge to the Bronzekeller, a cabaret on Carl Muck Platz where the artists had retained a lot of political courage and performed from the heart. None of their numbers approximated to the type of entertainment favored by the Nazis, and they still used satirical material by Mascha Kaléko and Kurt Tucholsky.

At the Bronzekeller I got to know Otto Larsen, who had a big, well-lit studio near the Kleiner Jungfernstieg, with a view across the Alster. Very alert to the needs of the time, Otto manufactured decorative tiles. Articles suitable as presents were unobtainable, so he not only supplied them but convinced the citizens of Hamburg that their dearest wish was to own one of his ceramic coffee-pot stands or jardinieres. Once I had been taught how to mix and use china paints, I specialized in colorful fishing smacks with swelling sails and dainty Chinese maidens carrying parasols. We drew our motifs on greaseproof paper, pricked the outlines with a pin, laid the sheets down on tiles, sprinkled them with powdered granite—and there were the silhouettes of our boats and Chinese girls, transferred to the tiles and ready to be colored in. Waves could be imbued with movement by varying the pressure of one's brush. The work was enjoyable as well as remunerative, and some of the friendships I formed at the studio have endured to this day. It was there that I got to know Olli Cohnheim, who already owned the country retreat at Staufen where she put us up after the great air raid. I obtained a labor permit entitling me to pursue an occupation—though only in a "non-self-employed" capacity, of course—and when Otto Larsen was finally drafted and had to close the studio down, I continued to work on my own account. My customers among the storekeepers of Hamburg never asked to see my "Aryan credentials," and the local revenue office proved equally incurious.

7.19.40: *Jews are debarred from being telephone subscribers. Exceptions will be made for legal consultants, medical practitioners, and persons living in privileged mixed matrimony.* (P. 325)

90

My daughter Barbara was born on August 26, 1941. My father had wangled me into the Elisabeth Hospital, formerly a Masonic institution, and managed to get me a private room there. Anxious to avoid awkward questions, I paid the hospital fees out of my own earnings. I was very well treated in spite of my unmarried state. Nothing marred the tranquillity of my confinement except the early morning din from a neighboring slaughterhouse, which I found excruciating.

In those days, parents were issued lists of officially approved names. Children born in the Thousand Year Reich could not be given names from the Old Testament—Esther or Rachel, for instance. Much to our secret amusement, Maria was considered acceptable!

The delighted grandfather came to see me every morning, the youthful grandmother every afternoon. Caution dictated the strictest adherence to this schedule because we didn't know how closely their enforced separation was being supervised by Nazi informers, and Barbara's birth would have been an opportunity to catch them out.

My father adored taking the little "second degree halfbreed" for walks, though the preliminaries this entailed were elaborate in the extreme. Being a "legal consultant" and exempt from wearing a star, he was at liberty to use public telephone booths, so he would dial our number and hang up without speaking. My mother then carried Barbara downstairs to the lobby—we lived on the third floor—where she had previously left the baby carriage. She made her way cautiously to the front door, and when my father came into view on the corner of Hansastrasse and Grindelallee, she would trundle Barbara outside, dart back into the house, and wait till the two of them were together. The baby's return followed the same pattern. We had long ago ceased to chafe at the indignity of such situations.

Although I received a child allowance from the German armed forces, the arrival of a new little family member made it necessary for me to earn some additional money. The ever-helpful Rolf Sommer had cleverly contrived to get his business in Kleine Bäckerstrasse classified as "essential to the war effort," so I continued to work there half-days. The evenings—and many, many nights in the air raid shelter—I devoted to painting tiles. By now I was adept at balancing a drawing board on my knee and working in the dimly lit cellar. Looking back, I don't know how I managed to keep a steady hand when air raids were in progress, but the dull detonations we heard were said to be our own antiaircraft guns, and our part of the city wasn't hit until the summer of 1943. Until then, we seem to have preserved a strange kind of fortitude or fatalism.

My friend Ingrid also led a very difficult existence in Hansastrasse, where she lived with her little son Kai and her Jewish mother. I taught her to paint tiles, and we jointly pursued this colorful activity for a couple of years. Ingrid moved south to the Fichtelgebirge after the big raid, but not before she had braved the turmoil that reigned in the blazing city and procured her mother some false papers. They both survived the war.

12.19.38: *Permission for Jews and first degree half-breeds to change their names will as a rule be denied. (P. 269)*

One day in the summer of 1941, my mother received a visit from an official of some kind. Didn't my brother and I also wish to assume the name "von Sillich"? The decree of December 1938 must have escaped his notice. Wolfgang and I dismissed the suggestion, but I still wonder if we would have been quite so adamant if our surname had been typically Jewish.

I recall this incident in tribute to our friend Olli Cohnheim. Being only a "second degree half-breed," she might well have obtained permission to drop the name that had proved such a handicap, but she clung to it through thick and thin. Olli was compelled to close her Hamburg bookbindery because the "Cohnheim" frightened customers away. She ran a small handicrafts business for a while after moving to the Black Forest, but that eventually folded, too. When I myself moved south and mentioned her name to a prospective purchaser of my painted tiles, he told me that a Jewess's recommendation was no recommendation at all. In spite of everything, Olli never dropped her father's "suspect" name.

Incidental note: Germans of the younger generation are hardly aware that such a thing as a "typically Jewish" name exists.

10.24.41: *Persons of German blood who openly display their friendly relations with Jews are to be temporarily detained on educational grounds, or, in more serious cases, committed to a grade one concentration camp for a term of up to three months. The Jewish party will in every case be detained in a concentration camp until further notice. (P. 353)*

Wolfgang and I were not prepared to forgo our non-Jewish friends. As long as they had the guts, so did we. Although this seems a rather rash attitude in retrospect, we doubted the authorities could keep us under constant surveillance for years on end. Our parents lived in fear, but we had become inured to the idea that our life was a macabre dance on the edge of a volcano. Did we really have to spend every waking minute wondering when it would erupt?

Little Inge recalls:

"I was out walking with Rudi Samson, my friend from the 'Comrades.' We were strolling side by side down a narrow street to Rothenbaumchaussee—Turmweg, I think it was. Rudi was wheeling his bicycle. Two men in SS uniform came toward us from the direction of Reitplatz, and before we could dodge them one of them planted himself in front of Rudi and started brandishing his riding crop. 'You Jewish lout!' he said. 'This'll teach you to run around with a German girl!' Before he could lash out, the other one pulled him away. The 'German girl' was me.

"Rudi emigrated to Holland with his parents soon afterward and died in a concentration camp."

Ali had introduced Little Inge and me to some friends who used to go sailing on the Elbe from the yacht basin at Schulau, near Wedel. For us this marked the beginning of a pleasant interlude—our happiest in all those wartime years. Out on the Elbe we lost our dread of the ominous ring at the door before dawn, the Gestapo's favorite visiting time. Our new friends, who were all in more or less middle-class jobs, ranged from dentists and painters to technical draftsmen. United in their hatred of the Nazis, they were always ready to take us along, help us, take our mind off things, give us a good time.

I learned to play the concertina, cook Chinese food, and bring myself to eat fish that had been hooked and gutted before my eyes. Those weekends on the water helped us a lot. They were aids to existence denied to our parents.

During one such weekend, Little Inge had a tragicomic experience:

"It happened in the train from Wedel to Hamburg. I and an equally blonde girlfriend had come straight off the boat and boarded the train in our blue ducks and white summer blouses.

It was sweltering hot, and we'd grabbed two corner seats. The section was jam-packed with yachting cronies and tourists. Suddenly we heard a man say, 'Disgraceful of two BDM girls to go on sitting there while older folk have to stand!' There was a silence. Then my girlfriend's half-Jewish husband cleared his throat and growled, 'Quite right, you BDM girls ought to know better!'

"That was when we still had the courage to joke about things."

Another of Little Inge's reminiscences:

9.18.41: *Jews are entitled to use . . . public transportation only when there is room for them, but not during rush hours, when even some non-Jewish passengers cannot be accommodated. Jews are restricted to second- and third-class travel and may occupy seats only when no other travelers are standing. (P. 350)*

"We were in a streetcar. My father had to stand on the step. The two of us rode down Mittelweg together, I so perfectly attuned to 'master race' notions with my blonde hair and blue eyes, and my poor, dejected father. I was eager to see what would happen. Nothing at all. One or two fellow passengers eyed us curiously, others sympathetically, but no one said anything or looked aggressive."

We existed in a peculiar limbo, torn between fear, suspense, and curiosity. How else could we have endured life, if not as students of the world around us?

95

HARASSMENT AND FOREBODING

(1942)

1.3.42: *In view of the impending final solution of the Jewish problem, emigration from the Reich by Jews of German nationality and stateless Jews is hereby discontinued. . . . (P. 361)*

THE WANNSEE CONFERENCE, which approved the Final Solution, was held on January 20, 1942.

On July 9, 1942, Little Inge's father received an ominous summons to report to Hartungstrasse with one suitcase and the money for his fare. While en route he managed to write a postcard whose wording implied that it had been smuggled off a train. "We're heading east," it said.

That was the last she ever heard of him.

The first major exodus of deportees from Hamburg in October 1942 was witnessed by my former schoolteacher Elisabeth Flügge. Here is how she recalled one particular incident:

"I happened to be calling on a very refined old lady who had been unable to emigrate because of her frail physical condition and was now languishing in one wretched little room. Suddenly we heard a voice on the stairs: 'Everyone to the assembly center' (the Masonic lodge at Moorweide) 'by eight A.M. tomorrow!' She thereupon begged me to strangle her with a towel. I told her I couldn't do that. I cycled off to see the German Red Cross and the leaders of the Jewish community, but they could only advise me to help her pack. The next day the house was deserted and the front door sealed, but I managed to discover that the old lady had been taken to a home for the aged on Bornplatz, and there she died."

I last saw another ex-teacher of mine, Fräulein Angerstein, not long before the first big raid on Hamburg in 1942. She was very ill—suffering from muscular dystrophy. Her head had retained its normal shape, but her arms were terribly withered. Although she could no longer move her shrunken hands, she consoled herself with the literature she loved so much. Propped up behind a book rest, she would wait patiently for a nurse to come and turn the page for her. I told her about Barbara's birth. These days, she said, she wouldn't wear a swastika pin. . . .

Jews destined for deportation could leave their money to "semirelated" members of the family who were staying behind in Germany, but not to "full Jews," meaning any of their children who had emigrated.

My brother and I were accordingly named as her heirs by our great-aunt, Jenny Rosenmeyer, the last surviving sister of our paternal grandmother and Uncle Adolf Calmann (the doctor who had brought us into the world). Her son Kurt had emigrated to London, her daughter-in-law and the grandchildren to New York. She, being old and sick, could not obtain an entry visa to any foreign country.

We didn't want the money, but Father pointed out that we couldn't touch it anyway because it was held in a blocked account and would remain there for the foreseeable future. This way, he said, there was at least a slender possibility of keeping it in the family.

One afternoon Aunt Jenny telephoned us. "They're sending us off to Theresienstadt," she said in a tremulous voice. "We managed to buy places in a home there." She was then living in an old people's home at or near Blankenese. Little Inge and I went there to say good-bye. Aunt Jenny was braver than either of us, but it was a heartrending farewell.

These "home purchase deeds," I should add, were one of the Nazis' most cynical frauds, because the following decree was absolutely worthless:

6.18.42: *Home purchase deeds are to be prepared for persons who will in the future be deported to Theresienstadt....* P. 377)

Anyone interested in the subject should read Käthe Starke's *Der Führer schenkt den Juden eine Stadt*, published in 1975. How people wound up in Theresienstadt, which was Hitler's attempt to convince foreigners of his humanity, and how they "lived," vegetated, and died there, is a macabre theme in its own right. There were no gas chambers, just starvation and disease and harassment in all its infinitely humiliating forms. For most of the inhabitants, Theresienstadt was a wretched transit camp on the road to extermination.

Aunt Jenny and the other old ladies from her home were assigned to a batch of deportees who never arrived. It later transpired that, in many cases, "gassing vans" were summarily put to work en route.

One tries to find retrospective consolation—if the word can be used here—in the thought that these old and under-nourished people, whose children were already safe overseas, and who dreaded the rigors of the journey ahead, may at least briefly have hoped that Theresienstadt would provide them with a new home in which to await the end of the war and an eventual reunion with their loved ones.

One reason why the infant Federal Republic of Germany made such heavy weather of Aunt Jenny's will was that a testamentary court in Hamburg wanted to pay me and my brother our illegitimate legacies in the early 1950s, even though the legitimate heirs had survived overseas. We managed with some difficulty to put things right, but our cousins across the channel and the Atlantic insisted that we share in their sad inheritance.

1.4.42: *Confidential. Further to the collection of woolens and furs for the eastern front, Jews are to be urged to surrender articles of winter clothing suitable for the front. Elders of resident Jewish communities must be informed that it would cause resentment among citizens of German stock if Jews continued to wear fur garments while citizens of German stock self-sacrificingly donated articles of winter clothing for the front. Jews will be expected to surrender such garments voluntarily, so as to obviate house-to-house searches. (P. 361)*

1.5.42: *Jews who are obliged to wear the Jewish star in public have until 1.16.42 to . . . surrender any fur and woolen garments in their possession. . . . (P. 362)*

These absurd decrees were bad for many reasons, not the least of which was an earlier sentence of hardship passed on the Jews in 1938:

2.14.38: *The minister of economic affairs announces that, in view of prevailing public sentiment, electrical and gas companies need have no qualms about excluding Jews by amending their statutes. (P. 216)*

This meant that German families wishing to harass Jewish fellow tenants could have their cables and pipes disconnected from the mains and cut off their power and gas supplies.

When we were visited after the war by a lady from Emmendingen who had emigrated to America, she gratefully recalled the kindness of some "Aryan" neighbors. Though unable to prevent her from being disconnected, they had drilled a hole in the floor and lowered an electric lead so that her "Jewish" baby's milk could be heated. That anecdote, too, deserves a place here.

In January 1942—the month of the "eastern front" decrees—my father brought me a fur coat belonging to a Jewish friend of ours. It wasn't an expensive fur, only a black sealskin, but nicely tailored. To me it seemed the height of elegance.

"I'm to tell you you're welcome to it."

I yearned to feel happy about the coat, but I did and I didn't. Spruce and snug, I was walking the wintry, wartime streets at someone else's expense.

Incidental note: it wasn't the soldiers at the front who attired themselves in Jewesses' fur coats. . . .

In the summer of 1942 our friend Ali, who had been drafted into an antiaircraft unit, was burned to death in an air raid on Hamburg.

THE FINAL REUNION
(1943)

10.7.40: *Although Jews cannot in practice be denied the use of air raid shelters, care must be taken to segregate them from the other occupants, either by creating a separate shelter for them, or by partitioning them off. (P. 327)*

A KIND OF MALAISE overcame me on the afternoon of July 24, 1943. I'd been fire-watching the night before, a regulation duty in all Hamburg office buildings, and the first shift hadn't been relieved till midnight. Was that why I felt so exhausted? After work Rolf Sommer took me to the Bodega on Rathausmarkt, where we sat over a glass of wine—a rare treat at that stage of the war—with Dr. Pschorr, his business associate, and Herbert Samuel, his attorney. For the umpteenth time, we debated our current preoccupations—in an undertone, of course. How much longer? Would we make it? Would we survive the bombing and the Gestapo?

My mother asked if I was ill when I got home. I couldn't say, exactly. Was it a presentiment of some kind? Edgy and depressed, I retired to bed early.

We never suspected, when the sirens started wailing, that we would never see our shabby, cozy old apartment again. It went up two terrible hours later, a bare thirty minutes after we quit the cellar. The building had been hit by a delayed-action bomb.

I would be exceeding the scope of my subject if I gave a

detailed description of our last night in the air raid shelter at No. 72, Hansastrasse. Suffice it to say that I sat there with the baby on my lap while my mother toured the two subterranean chambers, radiating confidence and sedating terrified old ladies with tincture of valerian. Every inch a soldier's daughter, I thought, admiring her self-discipline, because she was just as scared as the rest of us. The floor, the walls, the ceilings with their vulnerable maze of gas and water pipes—everything periodically shuddered and shook. From time to time my mother went upstairs to the janitor's apartment, where information and instructions poured in from some civil defense center for as long as the telephone system and radio station continued to function. Curiously enough, the Führer's female devotees—the ones who shared our floor of the house—had never observed or enforced the "segregation" decree. On the contrary, they swallowed my mother's valerian without turning a hair. I wondered what it must feel like to be ministered to by a woman who'd gone to jail because you'd denounced her. . . .

Then came the order to evacuate the building. We made our way in single file along a narrow, subterranean passage, emerged into the street, and headed for Hochallee. Take nothing with you and be quick, we were told. Only the janitor and my mother knew why.

In recounting what happened next, I shall abandon the tone appropriate to a memoir of this kind, which should strive to be impersonal and objective. The following account of my parents' last meeting, every word of which is true, appeared in Freiburg's *Badische Zeitung* as long ago as 1955.

I hurried along Hansastrasse with the baby in my arms, past rows of burning buildings. The whole neighborhood seemed to be ablaze. How in God's name had my father fared in nearby Dillstrasse, I wondered, and where was Wolfgang?

On and on I went, turning occasionally to look for my mother. She was lagging behind, toiling along under the weight of an old woman who was clinging to her and whimpering. Men in dungarees or civil defense corps uniforms stood outside blazing, smoking buildings. They signaled which way we should go by pointing and waving us on. Words would have been inaudible above the hiss and roar of the flames, the wail of ambulance sirens. Barbara's big blue eyes gazed placidly at the incandescent sky. Figures erupted from every door and hurried in our wake. We passed Ingrid's house, but I couldn't tell if it was on fire and didn't know if she and little Kai were still there.

At last the glare faded. Exhausted, I came to a halt. Mother and the old woman soon caught up, and we all perched on a garden wall. Behind us, ash veiled the sky like a gauze curtain. To left and right, seas of flame billowed high into the air. We were outside a corner house in Hochallee, where we used to live. A youngish woman came up to us, and we recognized her as Frau Schenk, our postwoman.

"Our place has a big cellar with emergency exits," she said. "We're laying out some mattresses right now. I'll let you have some proper bedclothes, and you can use my bathroom, too." We couldn't believe our ears!

The cellar was filled with exhausted people. Many were numb with shock, others quietly sobbing. Frau Schenk showed us into a little side room, provided us with bedclothes, brought us bread and steaming mugs of ersatz coffee. She attended to everyone's needs with the same angelic calm and deliberation. Somebody claimed to have heard the all clear in the distance. Our own sirens, which had evidently been destroyed, remained silent.

"I'm going to look for Father," I said, when Mother and Barbara were comfortably installed, and sallied forth into the night. It wasn't far to Dillstrasse, but I had to make several detours. There were signs of confusion everywhere—obstacles, fires, mountains of rubble. Members of the "master race" were accommodated in a concrete shelter nearby. The Jews of Dillstrasse, who were forbidden to set foot in this, had to retire to the cellars of their dilapidated old houses. Not for their own protection, though—far from it. According to the authorities, they had to leave their places of residence during air raids to prevent them from flashing signals to enemy aircraft!

Dillstrasse had been cordoned off. I could hear the shouts of firemen at work and the wail of fire engines racing to the scene, but the street itself was inaccessible. None of the houses had taken a direct hit, I was told, and I had to be content with that.

Frau Schenk was standing wearily outside her door when I returned. "Where on earth have you been?" she demanded. "Haven't you had enough excitement for one night?"

I leaned against the wall beside her. "I've been looking for my father. He lives in—in the neighborhood. My parents are divorced, but they're still on friendly terms."

"Better get some rest," said Frau Schenk. "You've a lot on your shoulders now." Was I wrong, or did I detect some special meaning in her tone? "And tomorrow morning you can go and get your father. Bring him here, then you and your mother won't need to worry so much."

Her kindly suggestion made my stomach turn over. Could we risk it? The Gestapo probably had enough to do without keeping track of us, especially now that our tracks had, in a sense, been obliterated. On the other hand, what if someone in the cellar recognized us? What if some Nazi harridan from the old people's home had found her way there?

Frau Schenk was a mind reader. "You're in the side room, aren't you? Well then! I'll put an extra camp bed in there, so say no more. Now go and get some sleep."

"For God's sake!" said my mother when I told her the wonderful news. "Are you sure it isn't a trap?"

Don't start crying, I told myself. If I started crying now I'd never stop. Our home was gone, but I mustn't cry.

"You only have to look at her," I said, though experience had taught us never to judge by friendly appearances. Even the people who had devised so many torments for us and translated them into law were kind to their friends and families, fed their canaries, fondled their dogs, and played Bach or Brahms. Not Mendelssohn, of course.

The house where my father lived had only had its windows shattered by blast. Plaster had fallen from the ceilings and walls, and the furniture and stacks of newspapers in his room were coated with a thin film of dust. At long last I could indulge in the luxury of a few tears of exhaustion and relief.

"The air raid warden complimented me." My father managed a faint smile. "I was up on the roof, putting out fires."

"Good God!" I exclaimed.

"You forget I'm an old soldier. I've been in action."

"Oh, sure, and you were trying to repay the fatherland for the privilege of climbing out of a Jewish cellar onto an Aryan roof!"

"They were all quite nice to us, the place was in such chaos."

I refrained from commenting on this acme of kindhearted

naïveté. Instead, I told him about Frau Schenk and her proposal. He echoed my mother's question.

"Mightn't it be a trap? I don't know. Just think, though, all of us being together at last. . . . If only Wolfgang would turn up, too!"

Wolfgang would see the ruins of No. 72, Hansastrasse, and assume the worst. Here at Dillstrasse we could only leave a sign of life, not a forwarding address. "I'll leave word at Little Inge's and the office," I said, hoping that nothing had happened to either place.

Wolfgang, who had spent the night at a friend's house, was at Little Inge's when I got there. He was overjoyed, because the sight of the ruins in Hansastrasse had filled him with the direst fears for our safety.

No one looked at us twice as we hurried through Frau Schenk's cellar and into the side room. "I brought you some cigarettes," my father told his divorced wife, as if they had parted only that morning, instead of being so brutally separated at Gestapo headquarters two years before.

He was playing with Barbara all the time. He produced a few cookies from his briefcase, together with a miniature bottle of brandy for me. Only someone aware of how drastically Jewish rations had been cut could gauge what it meant that he had still contrived to bring us each a little present. . . .

If I may be permitted, somewhat emotionally, to sum up this final encounter between my parents, I would put it thus: all their estrangement seemed to have melted away. There was no yesterday, nor would there be any tomorrow. There was just a friendly acceptance of the here and now in a stuffy little room lit not only by a candle whose flame flickered a trifle from lack of oxygen, but also by bright and affectionate memories of a past whose radiance was soon to be extinguished forever.

The next day my boss, Rolf Sommer, took us all to his house in Alsterdorf. From there he drove my mother, Barbara, and me to Lübeck, where we caught a train for the south of Germany. Our friend Olli Cohnheim had contacted us by phone via Little Inge and offered to put us up at her little cottage on the Rothof above Staufen, where peace still reigned.

Wolfgang remained in Hamburg with his girlfriend and wife-to-be. This meant that he was near my father, who went back to the unrelenting wretchedness of the Dillstrasse ghetto. It was typical of Felix Hecht, lawyer and old soldier, that he should have declined to leave the city with the aid of false papers. The authorities could not have checked up on him, at least for some time, but he was mortally afraid of exposing us to *Sippenhaft*, the Nazis' revival of a primitive Germanic law under which an entire family could be punished for the actions of one of its members.

My brother and I are still haunted by the thought that we failed to talk him into going—failed to stand by him like Ingrid, who saw to it that her mother survived the war under the pseudonym "Frau Meier." The loneliness he felt after our departure was only slightly mitigated by Wolfgang's future parents-in-law, who courageously helped him whenever they could.

After the war, when I traveled from Freiburg to Hamburg for a reunion with Wolfgang, the first thing I did was to call on Frau Schenk. It transpired that she had known all about us. "I used to deliver mail to Dillstrasse, too," she explained. "That's why I gave you the side room when you landed up here."

I was almost speechless with gratitude and admiration. "But weren't you scared of helping us like that?"

"Not that I remember," she said. "Everything was in such chaos. Anyway, even if I had been scared, what would my fears have been compared with yours?"

113

THE WAR YEARS
(1 9 4 3 – 1 9 4 5)

12.18.43: *Jews whose mixed marriages have been dissolved (hitherto exempted from wearing the Jewish star) and persons of formal Jewish status [Geltungsjuden] are to be sent to Theresienstadt. (P. 401)*

I SHUTTLED TO AND FRO between Staufen and Hamburg until Rolf Sommer evacuated his firm from the battered city to Marktredwitz, in Bavaria. He was going to let me know when his business had been allocated premises large enough to accommodate me, too. Instead, I was notified as follows:

"10.16.43. I regret to inform you that I cannot employ you for the time being. My reasons can only be communicated by word of mouth. . . ."

Dr. Pschorr received an identical letter. Sommer's Nazi clerk had stepped up the pressure. . . .

So I was unemployed. Herr Ilch, the mayor of Staufen, refrained from questioning me too closely. Although he was a Party member, he allowed me to do secretarial work at the town hall. They knew me there because I was always borrowing back numbers of the *Staufener Wochenblätter* from Herr Dufner, the town clerk. These contained articles on local history that I used as aids to familiarize myself with my new, adopted home.

We had managed, after making one or two detours, to

acquire a haven in the old granary on Marktplatz: one large room which we divided into two with wardrobes and closets. There was no running water—that we had to fetch from a fountain in Freihofgasse, opposite the side entrance—but we did have two handsome tiled stoves. My mother had learned how to stoke small cast-iron stoves during our stay with Olli on the Rothof, but tiled stoves? Although we were assigned a ration of logs, these were dumped in Freihofgasse, a narrow alleyway, and had to be split and toted upstairs. There was a chopping block on the Marktplatz side, but my vain attempts to wield an ax must have looked so pathetic that Emil Gutmann, another of the town hall clerks, put a stop to them. He solved our problem in short order by splitting the logs himself and teaching us how to stoke the stoves properly. It so happened that the OG, or local Party boss, lived on the top floor of the town hall, so he could see what was going on in the medieval marketplace below. One day he gave vent to the following pronouncement: "Fancy a German and a Party member chopping wood for a *Jewess* with a Party-owned ax!"

Fortunately, the OG never did more than attack us verbally—for instance to Fräulein Gysler, who owned the Freihof facing the granary. A fine old building designed by Peter Thumb, the celebrated eighteenth-century architect, the Freihof had once enjoyed the right of asylum. Fräulein Gysler, who still took this seriously, offered us shelter in its stout cellars when Allied aircraft flew over the little town, as they did with increasing frequency. Evidently conversant with the segregation order, the OG urged her to exclude us from her protection. Fräulein Gysler refused point-blank. She was a loyal German, she told him, but she didn't equate loyalty with inhumanity. It wasn't until much later that I learned of this courageous retort.

Where the treatment of "half-breeds" was concerned, the

118

authorities had exhibited differences of opinion as early as 1935. They were uncertain of our place in the scale of racial values, which may explain why no proceedings were taken against me on account of Barbara's birth. As time went by, however, interpretations of the Nuremberg Laws increased in stringency until, by the end of 1943, the outlook for partners in mixed marriages and for us, their children, was extremely ominous. Alois Schnorr, a Staufen bank manager who subsequently became finance minister of the little state of Baden, was arrested not long before the war ended. His Jewish wife was hidden by friends; his "half-breed" children were ostracized in the school playground by order of their teacher, Herr F., who also happened to be the aforesaid local Party boss.

Back in Hamburg, my father paid sporadic, halfhearted visits to the Honduran consulate to inquire about the current immigration quota.

On January 18, 1944, he gave my brother a handwritten postcard: "I hereby assign my son, Wolfgang Hecht of Hamburg 13 . . . power of attorney. This entitles him to take all requisite steps in my behalf. It shall not be rendered void by my death. Dr. Felix Israel Hecht." He had received his dread summons.

Neither of them let us know. Wolfgang didn't call Staufen until the train had departed on its sinister journey. He had escorted Father to the Talmud Torah School on Grindelhof and left him there with sixty other companions in misfortune. They were the fifteenth batch of deportees from Hamburg. Their destination: Theresienstadt.

Until 1942 we had never even heard of this former Austro-Hungarian fortress in Czechoslovakia, midway between Dresden and Prague. Now, its name was to be imprinted on our memories forever.

4.5.42: *Police commissioners, district administrators, and mayors of the Lower Rhine area are instructed not to enter the destination of consignments [of deportees] in their records. They are simply to mark them "Gone away, whereabouts unknown" or "Emigrated." (P. 369)*

This monstrous though altogether logical directive probably applied to the inmates of Theresienstadt as well, but at least their relatives received news of them. Theresienstadt was a deportation center that the Nazis used in an attempt to feign humane treatment of the Jews, principally for the benefit of foreigners. Foreign delegations were admitted, though their visits were stage-managed to a degree that put Potemkin's villages in the shade.

My father sent his first card from Berlin: "Dear children, everything has gone uneventfully so far. We're due to arrive about seven. Then we'll have to wait and see what happens." At Theresienstadt he met up with his sister Aunt Alice, who had been there since 1942 with her charges from the old people's home in Berlin.

The town was still divided into grid squares when my father got there. Street names were added later, so his "L 6" became Wallstrasse and "L 3" was christened Lange Strasse. To prevent the development of even a semblance of settled existence, no one was allowed to "live" in the same place for very long. The cold, bleak barrack rooms were usually crammed with people, all of whom had just as much space as their physical stature required. The boundaries of these "ubications" were staked out with their belongings, in other words, a suitcase and a heap of clothes.

Slightly more space was allotted to elderly men who had once made a special contribution to the life of the country that now disowned them. Academics for the most part, they were privileged to share one largish room with several of their number.

Although deportees were forbidden to receive "money and gift parcels of any description," there were many things that could be sent to Theresienstadt. We had little enough to send, however, and the preprinted reply cards were tersely worded: "Theresienstadt,_____1944. I gratefully acknowledge receipt of your parcel dated_____1944. Signed_____."

Inmates were permitted to preface these cards with the words "My dear" (or something similar) and add postscripts such as "I'm well—the jam and potatoes tasted wonderful" or "Very thoughtful of you to put in some shoe polish and shoe-laces." The latter were disguised requests, and we responded at once by sending off jam and potatoes, shoe polish and shoe-laces. Parcels being subject to a weight limit, the amount of food that could be sent—potatoes, for example—was pitifully small but vitally important nonetheless. When my father wrote under another name, as he did from time to time, we knew that a fellow deportee with no family had bequeathed him his monthly mail ration.

It was sometimes possible to write at greater length: "June 1, 1944 . . . Thank you first of all for the parcels, which have been arriving almost daily of late. I was very pleased with the contents, especially the rolled oats and the onions. They arrived safely because they were securely wrapped and strung. I can well believe that Barbara is progressing and endearing herself to everyone as much as you say. Inge is quite at liberty to enclose a picture of the child in her letter. She'll be three in August, so her little face must have changed a great deal. . . ."

On July 14, 1944, we received a card signed "Lutz Helischkowsky." It read: "Wolfgang's parcels of lard and canned vegetables arrived safely. Aunt Alice is managing all our cooking very well. She's still working for the health service, just as Pappi is still working as a lawyer. He has also taken over the running of a library, which suits him perfectly, as you can imagine, and gives him special pleasure. The weather here has been mostly fine. Apart from *Tosca* . . . we've been to a dress rehearsal of *Cyrano de Bergerac* and heard a lovely Mozart piano concerto, also some scenes from Ibsen's *Nora* and *The Lady from the Sea.* . . ."

Sometimes, for self-defensive reasons, we allowed ourselves to be lulled into a false sense of security by glowing reports of this kind. Opera? Concerts? Plays? The explanation emerges from Käthe Starke's book on Theresienstadt. Most performances like the ones mentioned—recreational activities pursued by people living in hopeless isolation but reluctant to abandon hope—were laboriously cobbled together by scholars who had filled their baggage with books instead of the practical necessities of life; either that, or enthusiasts combed the libraries, of which there were several, for musical scores and theatrical scripts. The *Cyrano*, for instance, was just a play reading which "for various Theresienstadt reasons" never got beyond the rehearsal stage.

We didn't dare publicize our connection with Theresienstadt, so Wolfgang used to forward Father's postcards in sealed envelopes. At first we naïvely believed that no one in Staufen would ever discover our personal circumstances. I now know how our particulars found their way so promptly to Gestapo headquarters at Lörrach. They were sent there in compliance with a directive issued long before the war:

9.6.35: *A Jewish file is to be opened, covering all Jews throughout Germany. (P. 126)*

Our identification was child's play, therefore, and made even easier by a subsequent, additional request from Gestapo headquarters at Karlsruhe:

11.6.40: *Secret State Police [Gestapo] offices are instructed to keep a record of Jews and half-breeds. (Three files: full Jews, first degree half-breeds, and persons of German blood professing the Jewish faith.) (P. 329)*

I mentioned that we had to make one or two detours before settling down in the old granary. There we could do as we pleased, but the same could not be said of our previous quarters. We'd had to be very discreet for the sake of a landlady who accommodated my mother and Barbara in the town, thereby sparing them a long and arduous trek from the Rothof, which stood in mountainous seclusion. We shall never forget the political courage she displayed in accepting us as lodgers. At the same time, we did have to contend with certain other difficulties that made it necessary for us to find a summer retreat somewhere outside town. A friendly family named Bob had a tennis pavilion and swimming pool in the middle of the verdant Etzenbach Valley, and this they put at our disposal. The "pavilion" was just a shack containing one small, oval room and a cellar. We often moved the local inhabitants to laughter by disappearing into the cellar at the first sound of aircraft, even though we realized that this small repository for tennis rackets would protect us from splinters at most. They stopped laughing after February 8, 1945, when the little town was devastated by Allied fighter bombers.

We spent many happy hours in the shack, I painting tiles and bookmarks, my mother manufacturing rather shapeless dolls out of old stockings and scraps of material. They all found a ready market, and I built up a faithful clientele among the stationers of Freiburg, who had no fountain pens or writing paper left to sell.

To refugees from a bomb-blasted city, the Etzenbach Valley was pure delight. We drank in the Black Forest air with gratitude, well aware of our good fortune. Then, one day, we were spotted by the OG, who kept his beehives nearby. There was something ominous about his habit of peering across at us. "He's got the evil eye," I said, and I was right. Friendly neighbors advised us not to provoke him by parading our cheerful, unconstrained existence before his eyes. Our move to the granary came none too soon.

This, incidentally, was around the time when the "September consignments" left Theresienstadt for Auschwitz, but of that we were still in ignorance. We merely wondered, with deep foreboding, why the flow of postcards had abruptly ceased.

On April 5, 1944, my brother Wolfgang was drafted for forced labor.

On October 10, 1950, the Hamburg Reparations Office declined to pay him compensation for wrongful imprisonment, a legal entitlement, on the ground that "no deprivation of liberty akin to imprisonment can be ascertained." Wolfgang commented on the decision to Herbert Samuel, who was representing him, in a letter dated March 28, 1951:

"Setting aside this very flimsy argument, it is unjustifiable and contrary to the spirit of the law to reject my claim while approving those of sundry acquaintances who worked alongside me in the same detachment. I realize that courts in various places have arrived at contrary conclusions in the same matter, but I feel that such things should not be allowed to happen in these reparation cases."

We often wondered, as the years went by and reparation proceedings dragged on, where and how the officials authorized to rule on such cases had lived during the Third Reich. . . . In Wolfgang's case the ruling was reversed on November 26, 1951, after he had submitted the following account of his experiences:

"Our so-called liability to forced labor was merely part of an extermination campaign, as the records of the Central State Security Bureau prove beyond doubt. . . . We had to assemble every morning in the gymnasium at Altona, where we were detailed for duty by squad commanders v. H. and B. I was in District 7. After morning parade . . . we were assigned work and had to march to the site in detachments, sometimes guarded by uniformed SA men. Our work consisted exclusively of strenuous manual labor, to which I and many of my friends were quite unaccustomed. I had been drafted from Glassmanufaktur Paul Besser of Altona, where I was a trainee clerk. We were paid the lowest possible wage (an unskilled laborer's rate) and were not entitled to . . . vacations or accident insurance . . . nor to any free time. We had to be on call day and night, and were obliged to report to Altona immediately after every air raid on Hamburg, nights and Sundays included. I spent many Sundays on duty, performing the following tasks: salvaging girders; demolishing buildings; retrieving corpses; carrying furniture and utensils out of bomb-damaged houses; stringing up power cables; repairing water mains; unearthing mains by shoring up bomb craters in snow and rain; salvaging bomb-damaged machinery; shoring up walls (at the risk of our lives, because hardly any of us knew how to handle girders or machinery without bringing rubble down on us); shoveling coal; emptying ashcans; and constructing anti-tank ditches with . . . prisoners of war and concentration camp detainees.

"The following quirk of fate may serve to illustrate our sense of insecurity. We had been detailed to dig some antitank ditches just beyond Harburg with a detachment of some ten Germans and sixty Italian prisoners of war. Five of my comrades were distraught because they had been ordered, out of the blue, to report the next day to a camp at Harburg-Wilhelmsburg commanded by a then notorious SS officer. We were in a state of utter consternation, because that meant being confined to barracks. Toward midday, Harburg sustained a severe and unheralded air raid. Not being accommodated in an air raid shelter, we and the prisoners spent the entire raid lying in the open between two antiaircraft batteries, which were later blown to pieces. We reached the construction site after marching for hours, and had occasion to note that the said camp had also been destroyed in the raid. . . .

"Because of my inexperience at lifting heavy weights, I developed tendinitis of the right hand, among other things. I was recalled two weeks later and assigned to District 1 soon afterward. I now had to parade every morning on Hegeplatz in Eppendorf under the command of G., a paver. At first the work was the same as before, but we later had to spend part of the time in Gross-Borstel PW camp, where we were put to work with Polish prisoners of war. The work there was generally more dangerous than in District 7, because we were employed in Harburg-Wilhelmsburg during heavy raids and not allowed to take cover when the early warning siren sounded. Most of our workplaces were fifteen or twenty minutes away from the shelters, so we nearly always got caught up in the raids. Air raid wardens several times refused to admit us to shelters on account of the Polish prisoners. In the case of the Wilhelmsburg surface shelter, in particular, we often had to dash inside during the panic that ensued on the dropping of the first bombs.

"I more than once worked twenty-two hours out of twenty-four at Harburg, where we had to repair railroad tracks in spite of continual explosions from the duds strewn around the oil refineries. . . . When sweeping streets and emptying ashcans, we had to report to a square near Haynstrasse, where we were detailed to assist employees of the Public Sanitation Service. Discounting the few assignments that enabled us to render people genuine assistance by digging them out of cellars or salvaging their possessions, the whole of our compulsory service was harassment, pure and simple, and we were powerless to resist our supervisors' oft-reiterated intention to 'put us where we belonged.'

"We were discharged on April 24, 1945. . . . I survived this spell of heavy manual labor relatively unscathed, except for a deteriorating knee injury. What I found worst of all was the constant mental strain and uncertainty. . . ."

My brother's knee injury still troubles him to this day. He ought to walk a good deal, having suffered a minor cardiac infarction, but it precludes him from doing so.

One of Wolfgang's fellow conscripts was Herbert Samuel, our attorney friend, and his first meeting with Ralph Giordano—they were both born in 1923—also dates from this period. Like Wolfgang, Giordano describes the parades on Hegeplatz, characterizing Herbert as a "once-prominent lawyer of the Free and Hanseatic City of Hamburg" who urged all present to maintain discipline and "comply with all instructions issued by those in authority over them."

Herbert Samuel, a universally respected figure, died on April 16, 1982. Wolfgang, who now lives in Latin America, described him in a letter to me as "a link with the past, and one of the last people to have known and been associated with our family's fate from early on." He also recalled: "When our squad commander greeted us in the morning with 'Heil Hitler,' Sammi's lone voice could be heard replying, 'And a very good morning to *you*. . . .' "

On January 2, 1952, Wolfgang was awarded compensation of DM 1,800 for wrongful imprisonment. In other words, his wages of fear amounted to DM 150 a month.

On February 7, 1945, I had to undergo an emergency operation in Freiburg while the hospital was under threat from low-flying aircraft. Though still very weak, I was sent home far too soon. The reasons for this were numerous and compelling. On February 8 the little town of Staufen sustained a heavy air raid that killed eighty of its inhabitants and destroyed forty houses. Blast had shattered the granary's windows and toppled our bookshelves. Everything was thick with dust—to our eyes, a familiar sight! My mother, who had been forced to neglect a bad bout of bronchitis, spent most of the time with Barbara in Fräulein Gysler's cellar across the way, relying on neighbors to cook for her. Things could hardly have been worse.

A Gestapo officer from Lörrach appeared on my first night home. Darkness had already fallen when we heard his boots come clumping up the stairs. He knocked loudly and demanded to speak to me. My mother swayed and leaned against the wall, assailed by memories of her time in Fuhlsbüttel Prison. I couldn't stand straight, far less walk. The man announced that I had been drafted, but my physical condition was obvious, and I also had a note from the hospital authorities certifying that they'd had to discharge me prematurely.

"I'll be back," the man said.

"Why?" I asked. "I'm the offspring of a privileged mixed marriage. That makes me half-Aryan."

The look he gave me was as unforgettable as his reply. "Half-Aryan? Half-Jewish, you mean, and that's as good as Jewish. Jews and Negroes, they're all the same to me." Then, "I'll order you to Lörrach three weeks from now."

"He forgot about the gypsies," I said when he'd gone,

recalling one of the by-products of the "blood preservation" law:

12.19.35:   *The only races in Europe to be regarded as alien are Jews and gypsies. (P. 146)*

So terror had stalked us to Staufen. Herr Dufner confided to me the next day that the Gestapo officer had called once before, but that he, Dufner, had "acted dumb."

I might have escaped the Lörrach authorities by setting off for Hamburg, but I was far too weak to travel. Besides, I couldn't risk abandoning my mother and child to their barbaric notions of collective responsibility, so I stayed put. Three weeks later the gentlemen of the Gestapo had other things on their minds. As in Hamburg, so in Lörrach, they were doubtless busy destroying their files.

French troops entered Staufen on April 23, 1945, my mother's forty-fifth birthday. From that day on, the invisible walls that had been erected between us and "the others" could be gradually dismantled.

Gradually, but not easily.

Fear dogged Little Inge, too, to the very last.

"July 1944, shortly before the birth of my son Thomas, who was due in August . . . I heard on the twentieth that an attempt had been made on Hitler's life, and for a few short hours I hoped that everything would be safely over by the time the child arrived. . . . But it went on.

"After the baby was born, my days in the hospital were haunted by a constant fear of questions—Who's the father? Why aren't you married?—but the deaconesses at the Bethesda asked me nothing. Their manner was reassuringly affable and discreet.

129

"One of the many problems awaiting me was potentially lethal. When registering the child's birth, I would have to produce my own birth certificate, which showed that I was a *Geltungsjüdin* [officially Jewish], not a 'first degree half-breed,' because my mother had adopted the Jewish faith on her marriage.

"Under the law, I should have worn a star and been sent to Theresienstadt. So far, for some reason, my status had remained undetected because I was 'racially' no different from the so-called 'privileged half-breeds,' especially as I had been baptized with Big Inge in 1938. Having received a final notice to register the child, I went to the registry office early in February. I claimed that my birth certificate had been destroyed in an air raid—a bold assertion, because we had never been bombed out. The registrar, who seemed friendly enough, made a note of my (false) particulars. Two weeks later I received a summons from the Gestapo to bring them my 'Aryan certificate.' I was interviewed by a woman official. Just as I entered her office, she was called away for a few moments. I managed to peek at the folder lying open on her desk. It turned out that the 'friendly' registrar had consulted his files and reported me. I was curtly informed that I was a *Geltungsjüdin*, knew what that implied, and would be notified in due course. That could only have meant a deportation order. Alarming though the prospect was, I decided to take the baby and make a dash for the Allied lines. I had spun out the proceedings long enough, however, because at the end of February the Gestapo authorities in Hamburg started destroying their records. The British were very near by then, so I and my baby were spared the appalling fate that overtook so many 'half-breeds' just before the Nazi regime came to an end."

AFTERWARD . . .

THE NAZIS' LEGAL SUCCESSORS found us rather difficult to deal with. We found them even more so.

Hamburg had been occupied by the British, Staufen by the French. Although Wolfgang was unable to get his apartment in Harvestehude exempted from seizure—the British requisitioned whole streets and blocks—the French authorities proved quite amenable. The biggest problem we had to contend with for a while was an order to return to Hamburg. What, after all, would we have done there?

In 1948 I married and settled in Badenweiler, so my long and laborious struggle to stay put was over at last.

For Wolfgang, life after the liberation was harder. Week after week he went to meet the buses returning from Theresienstadt, but our father was never on board.

We later consulted one of the bodies set up to deal with the innumerable cases like ours. In 1948, three years after the end of the war, we received a communication from the Missing Persons Service of the VVN or Vereinigung der Opfer des Naziregimes [Association of Victims of the Nazi Regime]:

"Re Dr. Felix Hecht, b. 9.24.83 in Hamburg.

"Having consulted Prague on the subject of the above inquiry, we today received the following reply: 'Pursuant to your inquiry of 4.9.47, we inform you that the lists of our Evidence Bureau contain this note on the above-mentioned person: "Dr. Felix Hecht, b. 9.24.83 in Hamburg, last place of residence Hamburg, was . . . transferred to Auschwitz (from Theresienstadt) with Consignment Ev 1651." Persons aged fifty and over may be regarded as deceased.'

"We regret our inability to give you any other reply."

Wolfgang decided to emigrate and now, as I have already said, lives in Latin America. His first port of call—a somewhat macabre coincidence—was Honduras. Because he finds the act of recollection unendurable, he has tried to overcome the past by devoting himself to the present. He, after all, came closer to the Final Solution than I: it was he who accompanied our father to the assembly center and was obliged to leave him there. . . .

Reparation . . . For us, this dreadful word has never acquired full meaning because we were only—to employ yet another official term that we had to learn and comprehend—"indirectly prejudiced."

We embarked on a nightmare journey through the jungle of the reparation laws. The authorities, who were obviously overtaxed, overtaxed us in turn. (They still do, by the way!) Every aspect of the "indirect prejudice" we had so patiently suffered had to be proved and proved again—and again. The postcards from Theresienstadt were not enough. Neither was the declaration of death, nor were the notorious "Special Laws." The authorities insisted on letters, testimonials, and affidavits covering every last detail.

Among those who confirmed that I could and would have

passed my university entrance examination was Hans Wolff-heim, who had finally, in 1946, obtained a lectureship at Hamburg University. He amplified his official affidavit in 1956—that is how long it all dragged on—by writing to me as follows:

"It is true that half-Jews could matriculate on paper and under the 'law' until 1941, and the bureaucrats of our democratic system appear to take their cue from these regulations. The actual position was quite different, however. There is now a reluctance to acknowledge that everyone, from schools and their principals upward, was at pains to impress the Party authorities as being 'pure Aryan.' Woe betide any half-Jew who invoked the 'law'!"

I got the education grant provided by law, and Wolfgang and I were jointly awarded our father's legal damages for wrongful imprisonment. Calculated from the date of his deportation to his putative date of death, May 1945, these amounted to DM 150 for every month he spent in custody.

To demand proof of our father's loss of earnings would have been absurd, but we had at least to obtain affidavits to the effect that we had lived in comfortable circumstances until 1933. On July 5, 1954, our erstwhile lodger in Hagedorn-strasse, Dr. Weil, sent the Reparations Office a letter from London. Part of it read:

"You must know as well as I do that most attorneys from 'good' Hamburg Jewish families derived a substantial income from their practices. . . . As the son of a well-known antique dealer, Dr. Hecht must have been on a really sound financial footing. . . ."

My former employer Emil Todtmann wrote: "My wife, who paid them several visits in their apartment, could tell from the way it was furnished that the H. family must have been well off before 1933."

And so on and so forth, from one indignity to another.

On the subject of Barbara's birth, the Reparations Office received a letter from Wolfgang's group leader in the Paulusbund, Gerhard Wundermacher: "Women who could not marry in consequence of the 'Nuremberg Laws' are among those who suffered most. It may be in the nature of things that no reparation law takes account of the injury they sustained."

In Little Inge's case the Reparations Office came up with another bright idea, though her attorney managed to knock it on the head. Two days after her father's deportation in July 1942, she received a postcard from him, as I have already mentioned. In calculating the amount of compensation due to her, the office wanted to equate the date on the card with the date of his death!

We were stripped of our rights, denied the opportunity to train for worthwhile professions, prevented from building up a livelihood, forbidden to marry. We shared the fears of those who failed to survive persecution, but we also had to endure the shame of having fared better than our fathers, our relations, our friends.

We did not emerge unscathed.

TO REMEMBER IS TO HEAL
Encounters between Victims of the Nuremberg Laws

GROSSE HAMBURGERSTRASSE

BERLIN, 1988. FRIENDS from the Brandenburg village of Brielow asked me rather circumspectly whether I would like to visit Grosse Hamburgerstrasse again now that fifty years had passed.

A wide entranceway led to a little public park. At one time there had been a Jewish cemetery here and a Jewish old people's home where I had visited my aunt Alice before Kristallnacht, the "Night of Broken Glass," November 9, 1938.

We stood in front of a monument: a group of twelve figures cast in shimmering gray bronze—emaciated, upright, frightfully isolated figures with features devoid of hope.[1]

Since tulips thrive in the village of Brielow, I took some with me and placed them at the feet of the gray figures. Afterward I noticed that other flowers, now wilted, had been laid in front of the few gravestones that were set into the cemetery walls. It was comforting to know that people still visit these graves from time to time.

We proceeded to the most famous of the former burial sites—that of Moses Mendelssohn—and began talking to some of the visitors.

"Are you familiar with Heinz Knobloch's book *Herr Moses in Berlin?*" someone asked me.

"No," I replied. So after I returned to Freiburg I made it a point to read the story of Herr Moses and how he had gone to Berlin in 1743 at the age of fourteen. Knobloch's narrative about this close personal friend of the dramatist Lessing, this Orthodox Jew and philosopher who had inaugurated the emancipation of German Jewry, begins in the very park where I had placed those red tulips:

> *Be suspicious of public parks. That tract of land on Grosse Hamburgerstrasse which in our innocence we regard as a little municipal park was once Berlin's oldest Jewish cemetery. The Gestapo sought to obliterate it from the face of the earth. . . . In a well-shaded area . . . there are some very old gravestones set into the cemetery wall. . . . They have been standing here for at least 200 years. Standing shoulder to shoulder, as it were, squeezed close together and seemingly unassailable, they look like soccer players guarding a goal against a free kick—a defense formation that is actually called a* wall. *This was the only reason these gravestones, the Hebrew inscriptions on which we were unable to read, had withstood the Gestapo's onslaught.*[2]

Senior citizens walked up and down the street in indifferent silence as I stood in the "little municipal park" on Grosse Hamburgerstrasse alone with my thoughts that afternoon. This was where the Gestapo had dug a slit trench, buttressing its sides with old gravestones—perhaps ones showing a pair of carved hands held in position for the priestly blessing or displaying a butterfly, the symbol of the transitoriness of life—as they tossed out the bones of the dead. I had no idea back then that it was here that the Nazis had established an assembly point for those who were to be deported, nor that my father, my aunt, and many others of Jewish origin—nearly fifty thousand people in all—would take their last steps on German soil here before being herded into railway cars and shipped to the East.

"Be suspicious of public parks. . . ."

NOTES

1. The monument was built by Will Lammert in 1985.

2. Heine Knobloch, *Herr Moses in Berlin: Ein Menschenfreund in Preussen: Das Leben des Moses Mendelssohn*, Veränderte und überarbeitete Ausgabe (Berlin: Das Arsenal, 1979, 1982), pp. 5–7.—Trans.

THE TRIP TO HAMBURG—
ROLLING HOME

IT WAS IN 1951 that I first realized I had a phobia about leaving my apartment. The only reason I mention it now is because of the circumstances in which I would overcome it many years later.

When I received the galleys of my book *Invisible Walls* in 1983, a friend of mine in Freiburg, Margot S., helped me proofread them. "We simply must go to Hamburg for the prepublication party," she said.

"Hamburg? I can't even go to nearby Breisach without having a panic attack. Hamburg!"

A dynamic and rather-frenetic-sounding gentleman by the name of Wolf Brümmel worked in the publicity department of the Hamburg publisher Hoffmann und Campe.

"If you decide to come, we'll host a reception after the release," he said. "And we'll not only invite the press and the media, but anyone else we can find who's mentioned in the book. We'd also be delighted to invite your friends from Freiburg. So what do you think? A good idea?"

"I think it's an excellent idea." However, I felt like adding, "It's totally out of the question." Then—as has become my custom over the past thirty years!—I promptly forget to voice what was truly an unreasonable reply.

I have a little radio next to my bed and like to fall asleep to the sound of music. It was sometime in December that I heard the strains of an accordion just before dozing off. For the first time in ages, I was treated to the sound of Heinz Reincke singing sea chanteys on the NDR radio network, direct from Hamburg—"my" Hamburg. I felt a pang of nostalgia.

Wolf Brümmel refused to take no for an answer. His voice became more and more persuasive. And Margot had her own physical therapy practice and a VW bus: "I can take a few days off. You should be able to manage nicely in my bus. Our bed is as comfortable as any in the Grand Hotel, and we have our own stove as well. The bus will be your home, and if you have a panic attack, all you have to do is close your eyes. The fact that your home is moving really shouldn't bother you. And if we get into a traffic jam, we'll make some tea. Or just sing."

The only traffic jams I had any knowledge of until then were those I had heard about on the radio. Later, NDR devoted another evening broadcast to nostalgic sea chanteys. "Come back soon, kid," one of them beckoned. So when I got a call from the gentleman with the persuasive voice who had so graciously taken me under his wing, I told him, "I'll come."

"Fantastic," said Wolf Brümmel. "Now the countdown begins."

José Barth worked as an editor for the Kerle Verlag, a subsidiary of Herder in Freiburg. He spent many an evening sipping a fine Markgräfler wine, reading those tentatively produced chapters of *Invisible Walls*, and bol-

144

stering my confidence in a manuscript that seemed to be going nowhere fast and might otherwise have ended up in a drawer or as a memoir for my grandchildren. In those days Germans still had difficulty confronting their past. At least now I felt that José was prepared to share in the work of remembering.

On February 14, 1984, I left my safe haven, and for the first time in thirty-three years, I ventured beyond my thirty-kilometer limit.

It is difficult enough to fight imaginary fears, but what about real ones?

As we drove past vineyards, meadows, and fields to the A5 autobahn, I began to engage in a strange conversation with myself.

My father, I said, had had to endure the journey to Auschwitz; could *that* fear possibly be described or comprehended? And here you are—going to Hamburg, where people are looking forward to seeing you, where they are preparing a party in your honor. . . .

There I was, sitting next to an upbeat friend, with José in the back favoring us with his marvelous gift for whistling classical music. Was he trying to dispel my emerging anxieties early in the morning with his rendition of *Eine kleine Nachtmusik?*

As we left the protective walls of Freiburg, my knees started shaking. What a prospect—1,800 kilometers and my knees knocking all the way to Hamburg. At least I had a harmonica to play if my anxiety level increased. The babe in the wood, rolling home. . . .

The only section of the autobahn I was acquainted with was that between Freiburg and Müllheim. I had always been told that the autobahn was a living hell. Whenever I heard reports on the radio—"stop-and-go traffic, gridlock, fog with a visibility of less than fifty meters"—I found it reassuring to know that those perils did not exist in my world. But then what did I actually encounter after we set off on our journey? First we drove along beautiful carpets of green turf, and then we whisked passed forests and meadows and mountain ridges; I never knew how lovely the bridges over a valley could be. . . .

"It's partly because of the bus," said Margot. "It's as if we were sitting on top of the world."

José was whistling Mozart's "Posthorn Serenade."

Then I realized that my knees were no longer shaking, and I finally started enjoying the trip. And did I ever enjoy it! "Live from the Frankfurt interchange," I said as we passed the sign on the freeway. I got a big laugh.

"Margot, José, am I dreaming?"

Margot pinched my arm. "If you can feel that, you're not."

Feel it I did. Sleeping Beauty waking up after her hundred years of sleep could not have been more amazed.

On our way north there was one place I absolutely had to see, even if it meant taking a detour—the little town of Bad Sassenbach. This was where the parents of my aunt Hanna, who immigrated to Shanghai in 1941, had lived. When my brother and I were children, we used to visit them and take the waters there. Since then I have always wanted to inhale that salt air again. Sassenbach was still quite rural back then, a lovely little resort not far from the medieval town of Soest. It was easy to find the spa gardens, but as I started out for the salt spring, I realized that regaining my health would not be all that easy. I did not want to get too far away from the car; it had become my home and my haven. . . .

"I thought you wanted to see the spring!" said Margot. "It's not transportable, you know." Margot and José got on either side of me. Shivers ran up and down my spine. We passed the bath with its dense saline vapors. The outdoor temperature was close to the freezing point, but visitors who were suffering from gout were bathing comfortably in the shade of the old saltworks—bathing in the waters I used to bathe in! For a moment my anxieties subsided and I felt a touch of nostalgia; I was pleased to see the spa again. It was along here, past this last vestige of an age in which brine was extracted from the salt spring, that we used to take our strolls—a little intact family utterly unaware of the future. Salt water was drained off the tall hawthorn hedges into a trough. Visitors to the spa would bend over the trough to inhale the vapors. At the thought of their inhaling, I suddenly found myself taking a deep breath. After sixty years I had come back—and for the first time after three decades I was truly on the trail of the past.

Margot wanted to buy some film; she felt we should record the trip in pictures. As I stood with her outside the photo shop, I had an idea: "Why don't you ask if anyone inside remembers the Janoschowitz family?"

As Margot emerged from the shop, she could not stop laughing and expressing her amazement. "It's incredible but true. There was a young man in the store whose grandmother worked in the home of your relatives until they moved away in 1934. The house, by the way, is over there."

Over there? The round staircase windows—yes, that might be it! "But it used to be surrounded by meadows and fields. My uncle had a nice farm over there with fields and cornflowers and poppies."

That was a long time ago. Like everything else.

Just outside Hamburg, where the autobahn passes through forests and heaths, I suddenly recalled the time I spent in the German Jewish Comrades' Hiking Association. The area around Wilseder Berg[1] is now part of a nature preserve, while the part near Osterheide has become a tank training ground where armored vehicles are allowed to ravage the earth. This was where we used to go on hikes: "Leaving gray city walls behind / we trek through forest and field." We passed the turnoff for Bergen-Belsen. On one of our next trips Margot and I would visit the camp.

We crossed the Elbe Bridges at dusk. A few months before, José had sent me a postcard with a picture of this very view, the view I had so longed to see. "I'm sure you'll see it again," he wrote.
And here I was now.
My heart was pounding.
There was a full moon over the Alster as we drove across the John F. Kennedy Bridge. The moon had been our loyal companion for one marvelous week, just as the sun had been during the daytime. Conditions such as these are far from the norm in Hamburg, especially in February.

My grandparents' house on Frauenthal—with its turrets, many corners, and bay windows— continues to exist only on the jacket of my book. It was torn down long ago. The structure that was built in its place has no sense of history; it had devastated the architectural landscape at the corner of what was once called the Klosterviertel. A stone's throw away is the "Hotel-Pension" at number 11 Nonnenstieg. It's my refuge whenever I stay in Hamburg.

"Little Inge," the second "protagonist" in my book and a friend since the days of my childhood and youth, was waiting for me at the hotel. The room was filled with flowers. There was also a large bouquet and a welcoming letter from my publisher.

"I still can't believe you're really here," said Little Inge. For thirty years she had visited me in my adopted city so that we would be sure to remain in touch. "Are we dreaming?"

"Not on your life," said Margot, holding out a newspaper that had been given her by the hotel manager. "When you've got it in black and white, you don't have a thing to fear!"

Her words sounded like a greeting addressed to Faust.

It turned out that what I had in black and white was the announcement of my visit—in the *Bild-Zeitung*, Germany's most widely circulated newspaper.

That was how my new life began.

My old school at number 90 Mittelweg was located nearby. The building now belongs to the university and has become a residence for some of the university's employees. As luck would have it, my friend Elsbeth Wolffheim lived on the first floor. Her husband, Hans Wolffheim, a professor of German language and literature, had been classified a "half-breed" and had spent those difficult years here in Hamburg with us. In 1971 he founded the Hamburg Arbeitsstelle für Exilliteratur (Study Center for Expatriate German Literature) and, sad to say, died two years later. Elsbeth had invited us for dinner. So just a few hours after having set foot in Hamburg again, I was standing, as it were, in my old school. I recognized the entrance, with its heavy door; the tiled floor of the stairwell was still intact.

As we entered the tiny dining room, Elsbeth said: "This is where your gym used to be."

The dining room included only an eighth of the old gym; walls had been erected to divide it into sections. When I looked out the window, though, I recalled how often I used to stand gazing into the distance and wishing for class to end. In my mind's eye, I could still see myself failing to do those dreadful splits as my gym teacher looked on unsympathetically. But since I could not stand gym anyway, I did not feel too guilty about my poor performance. The parquet floor where I had sweated so much because of my poor athletic ability looked unchanged; I swear I could still feel it under my feet.

Elsbeth brought some Greek wine.

"Welcome home," she said.

CELEBRATING THE PUBLICATION OF MY BOOK

Number 45 Harvesthuder Weg. A monument to Heinrich Heine stands in front of the old villa that houses the publishing company. I was profoundly aware of what it meant to be an author published by *his* publisher. And I must admit that when I walked into the building, I started shaking again. Wolf Brümmel accompanied me; the persuasive voice on the telephone had become a reassuring friend and helper who acted as if everything that was happening was the most natural thing in the world: the crowds moving among the colorful posters that covered the walls of the huge room, the life-size model of a British bobby standing behind the little table that had been set up for me. At just the right moment Wolf urged to me to try to enjoy the place and the people—they had come here, after all, because they wanted to read *Invisible Walls*.

"This is standard practice," said Wolf as he introduced me to the representatives of the press. The next day the

Hamburger Abendblatt reported:

> *The publisher had sent out invitations to afternoon tea. Among those who came were friends of her youth, former neighbors and teachers as well as others who are not mentioned in the book but share her feelings. Ida Ehre would not have missed this occasion for the world. The writer Ralph Giordano, who wrote the preface to [her] book, was also present. And why? Because Giordano and her brother had both been put to forced labor and shared a common fate. Surely reason enough for having become such close friends. . . . Ingeborg Hecht will remain in Hamburg for a week, strolling down familiar streets, feeding the swans at the Alster, and visiting friends. . . .*

The next day I read in the *Deutsches Allgemeines Wochenblatt* that *Invisible Walls* had been selected as the "Book of the Week."

My grandchildren Matthias and Florian, eighteen and nineteen years old, respectively, came from Berlin for the prepublication party. The only place they had known their grandmother until then was within the confines of her apartment in Freiburg. A number of my former classmates turned up as well, as did a colleague from the firm at which I had worked during the war (the head of the firm, Rolf Sommer, had had the courage to create jobs for "halfbreeds" within his company and helped protect them from persecution); our old youth group leader, Kurt, and his wife, Liesel, also made an appearance. The guests included a lawyer whose husband once came to our aid when our parents were arrested. Little Inge's teacher who had protected her from discrimination was there, too. I was espe-

151

cially pleased that Dr. Käthe Starke had decided to come. She had written a book entitled *Der Führer schenkt den Juden eine Stadt* (*The Führer Makes a Gift of a City to the Jews*).[2] This was also the cynical title of a film produced at Theresienstadt by the Nazi Ministry of Propaganda showcasing a city made up of nothing but facades, with sham events held to deceive the outside world about the real nature of the camp. What it actually showed was the Nazis' utter contempt for their victims. None of the actors or cameramen—not even the director—discovered the real purpose of this hideous fabrication because none of them was allowed to survive the filming. Only many years later were these details made public by the media; on March 20, 1990, for instance, the ZDF television network broadcast a documentary by Marion Schmid called *Der Profi—von der Traumfabrik nach Theresienstadt* (*The Pro—from the Dream Factory to Theresienstadt*) that chronicled the life and death of the director Kurt Gerron, a Berlin Jew.

Käthe Starke was the first person to give me a picture of what Theresienstadt had really been like.

My discussions with friends, members of the publisher's team, and journalists moved me deeply. Listening to my grandchildren being interviewed on NDR, I was surprised to learn that they knew as much as they did about the Third Reich. I credit the Berlin school system. When my grandchildren should have begun learning more about the Nazi period at home, their mother—my daughter Barbara—was no longer alive to instruct them.

My publisher had arranged something special for the evening. You may recall that in 1940 I was working in a printing house in the center of the Old City, on

Hopfenmarkt. I adored the place, situated as it was in the shadow of St. Nicholas's Church close to the canals. In my adopted hometown in the Black Forest, I had often longed to see the Old City again, to smell the aroma of the cocoa, coffee, and spices stored in the warehouses on Deichstrasse. And now my publisher had invited us to dine at the Nikolaikeller at number 36 Cremon.

I would never have recognized the area around the Trost Bridge if I hadn't had the charred steeple of that bombed-out church to help me orient myself. Located near the still unfamiliar Ost-West-Strasse, it rose into the sky like a memorial. (Ah, Heinrich Heine: "What will the lonely teardrop, / that troubles so my eye? / It tarries, a lone survivor, / from days long since gone by.") I was getting very close to Cremon when I recognized the building; it looked just as it had back then. However, I quickly realized that only the facade had been preserved. As soon as I opened the door, I saw that everything else was different. The interior had been completely altered.

In the old days, I used to take the elevator all the way to the top, to the studio apartment of my "Aryan" girlfriend who provided Little Inge and me with many uplifting hours as we sat looking out over the roofs of Hamburg, forgetting for the moment our fears and worries.

We walked down a few steps to the dining room. I cannot begin to describe how I felt after having lived happily for thirty-three years at the edge of the Black Forest and yet always longing to see Hamburg again. From where I sat, I had a beautiful view of the canals.

A portrait of the actor Hans Albers pictured in front of a colorful seafaring scene looked down on me as I sat at the end of our long, narrow table. Suddenly Albers started singing—on tape, that is—"Over here, boys, to *La Paloma!*"

Everybody around me was laughing. I was singing along with the recording. Everyone present toasted me, even Ralph Giordano.

As we were eating our lobscouse, Ralph told the assembled guests the story of our first meeting. When he was touring the country in 1983 in a chauffeured limousine provided by Fischer Verlag and giving readings from his family saga *Die Bertinis*, he made a stop in Freiburg. He had allowed himself an extra day to see me. Although we must have had many of the same experiences in Hamburg, it was in Freiburg that we actually got together for the first time. Ralph came over for tea and then asked me to show him the Markgräfler Land. I was somewhat upset by his request. He knew about my agoraphobia and the fact that I virtually never left my private refuge. Feigning surprise, he said: "But *I* will be there with you."

"Well, how did things proceed?" asked the long-suffering Wolf Brümmel, who had spent weeks on the phone himself trying to counter my arguments about not wanting to go to Hamburg.

Ralph raised his glass and laughed. "She got into the car, and we had a wonderful day in Staufen, Sulzburg, and Münstertal. It was my contribution to Ingeborg's recovery. It was, so to speak, her first step toward a new life."

Even now it's hard for me to believe that I actually got into that car with him.

"Ralph," I said that evening (and to this day I keep asking the same question), "do we have the right to be as happy as we are now and to enjoy ourselves, considering all the horrible things that have brought us together?"

"We do," said the author of the *Bertinis*. "We do, Ingeborg. We have said everything that we were obliged to in order to make sure that nobody in Germany forgets, and we've done it in memory of those of us who died—of all those who died. People are listening to us. For a year I've been privileged to learn this firsthand. And they'll listen to you, too. The dead would be the last to begrudge us these hours with our *allies*. "Allies" is what Ralph called Germans who were prepared to deal with their history and our history.

What Ralph predicted that evening came true: people did listen to me. If they hadn't, I would not have written this second book.

JOURNEYS INTO THE PAST

The writer Felix Rexhausen lives in Hamburg. He presented me with a copy of his book *In Harvestehude*. In 1978 he had been the official chronicler, as it were, for the Harvestehude district of Hamburg. He used to live on Frauenthal, not far from my grandparents' house.

> *I lived in the attic of a house that had been designed as a villa in 1882. If you discount the former "servants'" quarters in the basement, the attic constituted the third story. From the front I could look through the branches of ancient tall trees to a perfectly regular row of facades across the street; and slightly to the left I could make out the wide end of Frauenthal as it runs diagonally into Heilwigstrasse, just twenty houses away from the farthest point of the Aussenalster. From the back of the attic I could see the sky. The area between Frauenthal and Abteistrasse remained undeveloped for quite some time; it was said there used to be tennis courts there, surrounded by orchards. . . .*

It was one of those strokes of good fortune in my life that during my first few days in Hamburg I ran into someone who was able to describe perfectly the ambience of number 7 Frauenthal, where my father had grown up. My mother had once played tennis on those very courts "surrounded by orchards." It was in the basement of that house, in the big kitchen, that Little Elisabeth informed us that she wished to be trained in the culinary arts by our cook Marie. Elisabeth—nicknamed *Appelschnut* (Apple Snout) after the little daughter of the writer Otto Ernst—was seventeen at the time.

In the summer of 1983, Little Elisabeth, who lives in Jesteburg, got in touch with us; she had tracked us down through my book. Whenever I am in the neighborhood, I go to see her and her husband in their lovely little house, located in a bucolic setting surrounded by pine trees.

"There was a magnificent pine tree in your garden on Frauenthal," recalled "Little" Elisabeth, who had just turned ninety.

"My father planted it when he was a boy," I told her.

During these six days, I revisited almost every place I had wished to see again in the southwest of Hamburg: the city center and the Rathaus, the Jungfernstieg, and the Alster. Walking along the Elbe, I recalled how we used to sail on the river; whether it was for a weekend or just a few hours, we always felt so safe from the Gestapo (though not from Allied bombs) whenever we went sailing. And now the sun was shining, peaceful and bright.

Outwardly our house at number 73 Hochallee was unchanged; inside it had been divided into several apartments. This was a positive development in my eyes, though, because it helped me from being overwhelmed by yet more memories. The apartment house at number 27 Hagedornstrasse no longer existed. It had been hit during a night bombing raid, the other houses on the street escaping unscathed. The gap between the remaining buildings was quickly filled. The ordeal endured by my paternal uncle's family had taken place in the house next door, before they finally emigrated to Shanghai. My cousin Hans, who was eighteen at the time, described the trip to China for my book. It was in this house that they had been forced to consider the possibility of leaving Germany, well aware that homesickness would be their constant companion for a long time to come.

Cousin Hans visited me in 1990, and he and I went to see the house together. He filmed the site of his childhood, a childhood marred by racial persecution. He told his wife, Diane, and me the following anecdote: "A Luftwaffe officer lived next door to us. When the man was in the garden, he used to hand me chocolate over the fence, yet it turned out that this strapping officer was deathly afraid of running into me—a little kid—on the street. And when he did, he looked right through me, as though I didn't exist."

I was no longer able to rediscover the past where the house at number 72 Hansastrasse had once stood. Today the soaring Grindel high-rises dominate the area and the route configurations have changed. However, the section of Dillstrasse where the so-called "Jews' Houses" were located and where my father was ultimately forced to live was still intact, in the neighborhood known as Grindel.[3] In 1856 Grandfather Rexhausen, who resided in the posh Harvestehude district of Hamburg, noted: "Grindel is a collection of residences—not a community . . . the only positive element, the only thing that attracts me is the fact that there are a potpourri of Jews living there. I like being among people who have a different way of life."

After 1933, the people of Hamburg regarded such things quite differently.

I would like to jump ahead for a moment. In April 1989 I was invited by the Norderstedt Adult Education Center to give a reading. After returning to Freiburg, I got a phone call from a Frau K. in Norderstedt. She explained that in the early 1940s she had worked as a caretaker on Hagedornstrasse. Overjoyed at having found me, she poured out her memories. "I once took your cousin, little Hänschen, on a steamboat ride, because he wasn't allowed to walk anywhere anymore. A Nazi in the building promptly reported me to the police. But the matter didn't go any further because your family soon emigrated."

On my second morning in Hamburg, Little Inge and our youth group leader, Kuvo, and his wife, Liesel, came over for breakfast. We had not seen each other for almost fifty years, but during the prepublication party it had become obvious that our friendship was still intact despite the intervening alterations of time and place. In my book I had written:

> *Arrested and detained for some time, our group leader was released before long because his family had hurriedly made arrangements for him to emigrate. However, we now knew what a concentration camp was.*

"Last night we read part of your book," said Kuvo, whose real name was Kurt van der Walde. "It brought back all our memories: our hikes across the heath, our hitchhiking tours, our song."

We sat around the breakfast table in the sunlit corner where a bay window looked out onto the Nonnenstieg.

"Do you think we can still recall our song?"

Kuvo took a piece of paper out of his pocket.

"I spent half the night looking for it. And here it is: the 'Comrades' Marching Song.'"

The guests in the "Hotel-Pension" came from many different countries, which was only to be expected since it was surrounded by foreign consulates. There were actors and media representatives, photographers and musicians. The blue "Hotel-Pension" at number 11 Nonnenstieg, with its flourishing front garden and *Jugendstil* facade, is a Hamburg institution. The staff felt perfectly at home moving among art, kitsch, and kaffeeklatsch. And since they had seen it all—why not a couple of adult guests who felt like turning off their twenty-four-hour-a-day radios and performing something on their own? So we started to sing:

> *Hey, kids, why mope around home?*
> *When the sun is shining—why not roam?*
> *Why are your faces all so long?*
> *Can't you hear freedom's song?*

Even after fifty years, we did not complain about the fact that it was only the young who were being asked these kinds of questions. And as far as "freedom's song" was concerned—well, to be honest, the lyrics we recited with such enthusiasm were never very realistic. Many of our songs, after all, derived from the Youth Movement of the 1920s. We all still knew the refrain:

Comrades one and all are we,
decent types we aim to be,
on steep mountain paths follow our lead,
to the heart of life we will proceed.

"Our paths," said Kuvo, "certainly turned out to be steep. But did they lead to the heart of life?"

For some of those in our group, they led to death. For Kuvo, they led to emigration via a dreadful period of detention in Fuhlsbüttel Prison.

Nevertheless, our musical breakfast gave us a sense of joyful nostalgia.

My first public reading took place in the evening. I had been invited by Frau A. K. Michel, the owner of Sauermann's Book Store in Wandsbek, where Heidi Klessman was employed. Heidi's husband, Eckart, who had visited me during the PEN Club meeting in Freiburg, had read my book when it was still in manuscript form; he later reviewed it for *Die Zeit*. However, the invitation was not without its problems. I was still afraid to read out loud. So Little Inge's son Thomas lent me his voice—on the eve of his fortieth birthday. The date seemed particularly propitious because of the fact that my book virtually ends with the story of Thomas's birth, an event that could have easily resulted in his mother's deportation. (The tanks of Field Marshal Montgomery's Eighth Army ended up saving both her and her child.)

The introduction was the only part I could force myself to read; people could see the manuscript shaking in my hands.

The bookstore had an overflow crowd. And as I had feared, I was not yet able to maintain my composure in the face of my listeners' empathetic questions and emotional responses. I was still unable to present our story dispassionately. (Later, a young woman journalist was amazed that I was able to do as much as I did!)

When four gentlemen came over to introduce themselves to me, I had no idea that that encounter would revive part of the distant past. "We were members of the Ferdinande Carolina Lodge, the same one your father belonged to," they said. "In 1928 he was the Master of the Lodge." When my mother sometimes found a little relief from her cares and woes during those troubled times, she would say that the lodge had helped, though we never asked her exactly what she meant by that.

Now my father's memory would live again and go on living among the members of his fellowship. Miraculously, a new circle of friends began to take shape, one that included even my brother in far-off Central America. It was a comforting thought.

The evening before I left to return home, I saw and heard someone talking on the steps leading to the hotel, someone whose voice sounded very familiar. When the clerk at the reception desk greeted the gentleman, I nearly burst out laughing. It was Heinz Reincke. This can't be real, I thought!

"You know, in a way it's you I have to thank for bringing me back to Hamburg—my Hamburg—after an absence of almost thirty years," I said.

"How's that?" Reincke inquired.

In less than thirty seconds, I gave him a thumbnail sketch of my phobia and how his sea chanteys had helped me overcome it.

"What an absolutely delightful story," he said, and then he vanished.

I left him a copy of one of my books in which I had described the adventures of "a native of Hamburg living in Breisgau." They all revolved around the precious vine that plays such a wondrously "juicy" part in my adopted community—"blessed by the sun," as they say. However, in my dedication I got his first name wrong (Hans!). I hope he has forgiven me by now. After all, it had been some thirty years since I was exposed to the ambience of the Hamburg docks and the stage ship on which he sang his rousing sea chanteys.

After returning to Freiburg, I pored over reports and photos of that week in February. Down to this day, I believe that I was somehow miraculously restored to health in Hamburg. Here in the Black Forest, particularly in the little mountain and valley communities, religion is part of daily life. When people wish to give thanks for something, they bring an offering or a devotional picture of a saint to their church or place of pilgrimage. A native of Hamburg, though, does not have such a ready-made place to offer his or her gratitude. However, I did happen to have a collection box for the German Leprosy Relief Organization of Würzburg. (I had written a book describing how lepers lived during the Middle Ages, especially in Baden.)[4] We "half-breeds" had been reduced to the status of lepers in the Third Reich. Unlike us, though, lepers were not murdered in medieval times; they were merely banished and isolated from the rest of the population. Therefore, I'm sure that Sebastian, the patron saint of lepers, will accept my thanks for having had a wonderful trip during which I believe "invisible walls" started to come tumbling down.

NOTES

1. The highest peak on Lüneberg Heath.—TRANS.

2. Käthe Starke, *Der Führer schenkt den Juden eine Stadt: Bilder, Impressionen, Reportagen, Dokumente* (Berlin: Haude and Spener, 1975).

3. "Jews' Houses" were those in which persons with Jewish spouses lived.—TRANS.

4. Ingeborg Hecht, *Der Siechen Wandel* (Würzburg: Deutsches Aussätzigen-Hilfswerk, 1982).

"YOU WILL RECEIVE MANY LETTERS OF THANKS. . . ."

LETTERS FROM MY READERS AND WHAT RESULTED FROM THEM

IN JANUARY 1984, shortly before my book was published, Herr Biehler of the Herder Bookstore in Freiburg phoned me and asked whether I would like to give a reading.

"I'd love to," I said, "but unfortunately I can't." Once again I had to explain the meaning of agoraphobia. We came up with another idea, though. Since 1953, Freiburg had a theater called the Wallgraben (Moat), a name that seemed to promise a measure of protection. We asked the proprietor, the actress Ingeborg Steiert, whether she would read the chapters I had selected. She said that she would. I was very nervous as I entered the big bookstore. This would be the first time that an audience in my adopted hometown would learn about my family's history. As on previous occasions, I read the introduction myself. I was sure that everybody could see how much I was shaking.

After Ingeborg Steiert had finished, she sat down next to me. She was crying.

From that moment on each of us had a new friend.

"If they ever put your story on the stage," she said, "I want to play the part of your mother."

From then on invitations to give lectures and readings poured in. "Why don't you give the readings yourself?" was the question I was constantly being asked. In Voerde am Niederrhein, Little Inge's son once again stood in for me; in Sindelfingen and Heidelberg, Ralph Giordano and I read passages from my book together. We selected those whose tenor was in keeping with that of his novel; we had after all been subjected to the same indignities, "as decreed by law (in Nuremberg)."

It was during my reading tours that I really got to know Germany. Traces of the distant past often mingled with those of recent history. When we drove from Voerde to St. Victor's cathedral in Xanten, which had been rebuilt after the war, we found that candles had been lit in the crypt to commemorate those who had died at Auschwitz.

In Heidelberg I was given a book entitled *Das andere Heidelberg—Alternativer Stadtführer (The Other Heidelberg—an Alternative Guide to the City)*. I was shown the former Synagogenplatz, the monument in Rohrbach, and the memorial in the cemetery at Kirchheim. Since then I have often felt that I was never closer to the story of "my forefathers"—or to that of my father. Naturally, while I was in Heidelberg, I also visited the castle that rises above the city and looks down onto the banks of the Neckar River. My friends—Little Inge and Ralph Giordano—were always watching over me.

"The freedom to observe," said Ralph, "will restore the freedom of your soul. I think you should gradually try to give readings completely on your own."

Through my friends at the Wallgraben Theater, I made new contacts and formed new friendships. There was Berthel H., who asked if I would give readings from my book to the circle of acquaintances that regularly met at her home.

"If you can't do it, nobody is going to hold it against you. But it is an opportunity, after all, and it's worth giving a try."

Fortunately, I did try, and it turned out to be a success.

Why do I relate these things? Because I want to show that—to borrow a term used by German politicians in the 1960s—what helped me regain my health was a series of "concerted action programs."

The many positive responses that came from practically every quarter, even from the German-language media in other countries, caught me completely by surprise. After all, I was not one of those luminaries on the postwar literary scene who knew that whatever they wrote would resonate with large numbers of people. As a result of the success of *Invisible Walls*, a number of editors asked if I would review books that covered the same or similar subject matter. In spite of the psychological burden this activity imposes, it is still of the utmost importance to me. After many years during which the Nazi period had not been discussed publicly, bookshops began to fill up with documentary accounts of the Third Reich. I learned about the sufferings of others, compared with which mine seemed trivial. I read an account, for instance, by the physical therapist Simha Naor, a survivor of Auschwitz and Bergen-Belsen who now lives in Israel.[1] Though she describes moments of utter horror that can never be erased from her memory, her book still radiates that special kindliness that often comes with advancing years.

Then there is the following episode. During one of my readings, a sweet, elderly lady handed me a typescript copy of her autobiography that she had titled "We Must Never Forget: From the Life of Flora Neumann." A native of Hamburg, she wrote: "Based on our investigation, we are the only Jews in Hamburg to have survived the concentration camps as a family." Like Simha Naor, she too was a kindly soul completely free of hatred. Reading her manuscript nearly devastated me; I started having nightmares again, searching for my father. Until then I had avoided reading books about "life" in Auschwitz.

I began to hope that my father never actually had to see the extermination camp itself, that the SS physician Dr. Mengele had not directed him to the gas chambers as he stood waiting on the railway loading platform after arriving in Auschwitz, that he may have really believed he was being sent to take a shower. . . .

Please excuse me for not being able to keep these thoughts to myself.

Letters from my readers were among the many positive responses I received. As I mentioned earlier, I got to know my fellow "half-breed" Hans Wolffheim during the first year of the war; he became a professor of German language and literature after 1945. I told the story of how we met at some length in my book. After my book appeared,

I received the following letter, which gave me a special sense of joy:

Among the numerous letters that I continue to receive from readers, many come from my companions in misfortune and relate the stories of other "half-breeds." I would like to share some of them with the readers of this book, since the lives of those who lived between two worlds are still largely unknown.

In August 1984, for instance, I received the following letter from a clergywoman living in an Augustinian convent in northern Germany:

A few days ago someone sent me a copy of your book. . . . I raced through it at one go, almost in a daze. Then I reread it, slowly. I would like to thank you for having written it and especially for having written it in the way you did. . . . You touched something deep within me that I am rarely able to touch myself, though it is always there; in fact, the older I get, the more it makes its presence felt.

I was born in Hamburg in 1912 and obtained my high school diploma from a convent school in 1932. I then headed off blithely to study philosophy and theology at university. When the Nazis came to power in 1933, I found myself in a predicament for which I was totally unprepared—three of my grandparents were Jewish. I have no idea why I happened to be one of the 1.5%— that is the figure I remember—who were allowed to continue their university education. I studied general theology, was graduated from the faculty of theology at Rostock University in 1937, and got another degree from the Confessing Church in Berlin. I would never have been hired by a church in Hamburg and was reminded of the clergyman you wrote about who suddenly started ignoring you at school.[3]

With the Church's help I managed to get to England just in time, in 1939. I returned to Germany in 1946 as a parish priest. . . . "One's conscience can be pricked by the strangest little things," you write. How true. Why wasn't I—why weren't we all—more moved by what was happening to the Polish Jews living in Germany? Already in 1938 they were being driven back across the border into Poland.[4] Why didn't I try to prevent people from using the parish registries to document their "Aryan" ancestry? One of my duties when I worked as a substitute vicar in a small rural Pommeranian parish was to issue certificates of Aryan ancestry. Why am I even now unable to discuss this period dispassionately with my contemporaries (except for my close friends, of course)?

170

"We did not emerge unscathed," you write. Now that I am retired, I realize that almost more painfully than I did before. . . . Who is interested in what we suffered: unable to marry; cut off at a young age from anything that might have given us a little enjoyment in life; living in a state of constant fear. . . . I did of course have some positive experiences as well, both here and in England, and I will never forget them. I am happy that the Lutheran Church has finally begun the process of rethinking the past. It is hard to imagine all the damage done by the clergy.

I know that you will receive many letters of gratitude, Frau Hecht. Let me just close now by assuring you that I will pass your book on to others. Wishing you and your motherless grandchildren all the best, I remain

Yours sincerely,
G. F.

In September 1984 I received a letter postmarked Weil am Rhein. It came from a member of an organization that I would never have expected to hear from, namely an officer of the Wehrmacht:

I would like to offer my sincere thanks for your very courageous and "dispassionate" book. We—that is, my wife, who is "only one-quarter Jewish," and I, a "pure-blooded Aryan"—were married in 1940; however, we had to submit ourselves beforehand to a series of degrading examinations—which we passed—to determine our "racial makeup." Good friends and a bit of bluff helped get us through, but given my position as a staff officer, if the case had been reopened, it could have had dire consequences. Until the collapse of the Nazi regime, my wife and I lived under constant stress. . . . Your book recalled those forgotten, suppressed fears, but at the same time it had a liberating effect. We intend to pass the

171

book on to our children and other young people. Its unadorned
style should do more to help them gain an understanding of that
time than a recounting of endless horror stories. I sincerely hope
that it also provided a catharsis for you.

The final sentence in Dr. O.'s letter expresses a wish that has
been fulfilled in more ways than I would have ever dreamed
possible.

In November 1984 a letter from Jerusalem arrived:

I am a Jew who was born in Hamburg in 1911—in the very
clinic owned and operated by your great-uncle. And I lived at
number 42 Hansastrasse, just a few meters from your last place
of residence in the city. So I scarcely need to tell you the impact
your book had on me.

During the past few years I have been studying the history of
the Jews in Germany. Now I would like to concentrate on the his-
tory of the Jews in Hamburg. I believe that your reminiscences
would be very useful as I develop my project. Please write and let
me know what you think of my idea. I have been living in Israel
(formerly Palestine) since 1933, but I often visit Germany for
extended periods of time.

The writer of this letter, Naftali Bamberger, gave a
return address in Neuenburg, in care of a Dr. Barbara
Gehrts; Neuenburg is close to my hometown of Freiburg.
Gehrts's name rang a bell, so I phoned her. "What an
incredible coincidence," she said. "First of all, I am reading
your book right now, and second, Naftali is scheduled to
arrive here tomorrow."

We discovered that the reason her name was so familiar
was that I had heard it for the first time when the
Southwest German radio network broadcast a radio play

based on her book *Nie wieder ein Wort davon?*[5] The book had been awarded a prize for young adult literature. I was greatly impressed at the way in which she managed to describe those terrible times in a style suitable for young people. I might add that Barbara had personal knowledge of the period; she was just a young girl when her "Aryan" father was sentenced to death by the notorious Nazi judge Roland Freissler. Moreover, one of her schoolmates—a fifteen-year-old Jewish girl—had committed suicide after the girl's family had received their deportation orders.

A short time later, I met Naftali Bamberger at Barbara's bungalow, which is situated alongside a meadow near the Rhine. He explained that his father had been a rabbi in Hamburg at the Old-New Klaus Synagogue, which was located behind a toboggan slide in Grindel. His grandfather had also been a rabbi—in Sulzburg, of all places! A few weeks earlier, I had finished writing a book about this charming little village on the western slope of the Black Forest and its Jewish community, whose 400-year-old history had been obliterated in just a few hours on October 22, 1940. The Jews of Sulzburg were sent to Gurs, a notorious detention camp in the Pyrenees that was actually a way station to Auschwitz.

Since Naftali, though born in Hamburg, had a connection to the Markgräfler Land, he was able to provide me with additional information about the Jewish community of Sulzburg. "Since our paths crossed in such a strange way," he said, "I'm sure we must have played together at Innocentia Park when we were children. Maybe our nannies even put us on the same sled together?" Innocentia Park was close to Hochallee. Young people in the Black Forest would probably consider the little slope we used to toboggan down just a molehill. . . . I think Naftali was the first Orthodox Jew I had ever met. Incidentally, being unversed in religious matters had its pitfalls. One day my friend Doris and I—she did the illustrations for my Sulzburg book—dined out with Naftali; all of us ordered trout. The next day, Doris invited both of us over to her place. Smiling indulgently, Naftali politely turned down the salad. Doris had added some shrimp to give the fresh lettuce a taste of the sea. Later we found out that shrimp was not kosher and that not all aquatic animals had been created equal according to the Jewish dietary laws. Naftali gave us a short course on the biblical laws regarding food. I am sure my father had been taught these laws when he was young. He may have even observed them. I do not know why we never asked him about them. In any event, Jewish customs were not a topic of discussion before 1933.

When I was invited to give a reading to a group of mothers at the SOS Children's Village, I was delighted to find that they had decorated the little speaker's table for me and even included a menorah, with all the candles lit. "This is the first time," I said, "I've ever sat in front of a menorah."

In May 1984 I received a letter from Dr. Udo Löhr. As a public prosecutor, he had been appointed to serve with the Regional Appeals Court, the same court that had barred my father from practicing law in Hamburg. Dr. Löhr was also employed by the Professional Training and Examining Authority. He wrote me as follows:

For many years I have helped prosecute Nazi crimes of violence and have therefore acquired a special interest in the history of the Hamburg judiciary. When "Hamburg Justice Days" were organized in June 1983 by the Hamburg Judges' Association on whose board of directors I sit . . . we decided to show both the dark

*and the bright sides of the history of our legal system. A colleague
and I set up a documentary exhibit on the Nazi terror in
Hamburg. We called it "Justice under National Socialism." It
was very well attended, and we were pleased at the public's
response. At the suggestion of the chairman of the Hamburg
Judges' Association, Dr. Makowka, chief judge of the Regional
Court, the documents in the exhibit are to be put on permanent
display in a school classroom.*

*To enhance the visual impact of the exhibit, we wish to
include some photographs, and I have assumed personal responsibility for this part of the display. . . . Through your book I learned
of the terrible fate that befell your father and would very much
like to commemorate him in the exhibit.*

Dr. Löhr asked me for photographs of my father, his
birth and death dates, and the dates of his legal education.
But where was I supposed to get these things? We had been
"bombed out" during the war and, except for the papers we
had saved by stuffing them into a small suitcase—the very
papers I had used to help document my own background,
there was nothing left. Ironically, it was Dr. Löhr himself
who located my father's law school diploma and doctoral
dissertation in the Hamburg City Archives. My brother and
I owe him a great debt of gratitude. His son Tillmann, who
was ten years old at the time, marched into the Hall of
Justice, camera in hand, to photograph the display cases in
which his father had documented the life of my father. He
later wrote me a little note saying that he hoped I liked the
photos "and hoped they would be a nice souvenir." Oh,
Tillmann!

An incidental note: When I later went to see the exhibit (which was housed in the very same building in which

my father had worked as an attorney), I noticed a book in one of the display cases entitled *Streiflichter aus dem Hamburger Widerstand 1933–1945: Berichte und Dokumente (Highlights of the Anti-Nazi Movement in Hamburg 1933–1945: Reports and Documents)*. As I turned the pages, I was shocked to find the name of our youth group leader, Kuvo, as well as that of the German Jewish Comrades' Hiking Association.

As luck would have it, I had arranged to meet Kuvo at noon that day for lunch at a Chinese restaurant on Grindelhof. Little Inge and I were driven there by Dr. Löhr.

After the chop suey had been served, I asked Kuvo, "Tell me, who on earth from among the Comrades was active in the Resistance?"

He put down his chopsticks and, looking directly at us, said, "Almost all of them. We made sure that the youngest members, such as you, never knew what we were up to. We had to keep you out of the whole business."

"The Gestapo," I said as I felt my heart begin to pound, "would never have believed that we weren't involved."

I had good reason to be sure. Two years earlier I had received a book to review entitled *Weisse Möwe—Gelber Stern: das kurze Leben der Helga Beyer (White Seagull—Yellow Star: The Short Life of Helga Beyer)*.[6] I had gotten to know the author, Antje Dertinger, in Freiburg. Her book was based on the firsthand account by Helga's surviving sister. Helga had joined the Resistance along with several other members of the Breslau branch of the Comrades at the same time we were active in the organization. She was arrested and sent to prison, but instead of being released after serving her sentence, she was transferred to Ravensbrück concentration camp, where she later died. I repeated what I had said earlier: "The Gestapo would never have believed that we—Little Inge, the others, and I—were not somehow involved."

A year after I first met Dr. Löhr, Helge Grabitz, a senior public prosecutor, published a book entitled *NS-Prozesse— Psychogramme der Beteiligten (War Crime Trials in West Germany—Psychograms of the Parties Concerned)*, in which she profiled defendants and accusers, witnesses and victims, judges and experts. Born in 1934, she was obliged as public prosecutor, in the words of Simon Wiesenthal, "to seek justice, not revenge."[7]

We who survived cannot adequately thank her and people like her. Like our lives, her life will be forever changed by all that she had to hear and judge. In addition, her profession often involved her in examining witnesses in faraway places. Her little daughter soon realized how important her mother's trips abroad were.

"When I did have some time," Frau Grabitz said, "my daughter's school friends would come over and ask me to tell them exactly what was happening."

As I reported earlier, it was during my first trip to Hamburg that I got to know the generation of Masons that came after my father's. In my book I made specific mention of his lodge brother Dr. Fritz Ascher. Then in March 1984, I received the following letter from Thomas Held, a young social historian:

I was so excited by the publication of your book that I simply had to write you. My reasons for doing so are twofold. First, for about two years I have been corresponding with one of your friends in Hamburg, Frau Ursula Gaupp. In her last letter to me she referred to the bond that had developed between the two of you because of the fact that you are both "half-breeds" who had lived "between two worlds." Second, I am working on a social history dealing with the relations between Jews and Freemasons in Hamburg. I hardly need tell you that as I was doing my research, I came across your father's name. He played a not insignificant role in Hamburg's Masonic lodges.

What a fantastic stroke of luck: I had been trying forever to find out where Ursula was living; she and her mother had emigrated to Shanghai, and she was the granddaughter of my father's lodge brother Dr. Fritz Ascher. Now Thomas had fit the puzzle together.

A letter soon arrived from Pennsylvania where Ursula, her husband, children, and grandchildren lived. "There is so much I want to know about all of you, about our old friends," she wrote. Not long after writing me, she boarded a plane for Germany and arrived at my place. Things worked out particularly well, because our Little Inge was just about to turn sixty-five. Ursula's visit also happened to coincide with the first series of readings my publisher had arranged for me to give at bookstores in Hamburg. All this took place in April 1985.

Thrilled at having found each other again, we awarded Thomas our personal order of merit. Needless to say, it was the beginning of a new and beautiful friendship.

Dorle née Z. also came to celebrate Inge's birthday. We all recalled the time when both of them attended school together, which I had written about in my book. There was brave Fräulein Rieck (the future Frau B.), for instance. Dorle related the following:

> *After the promulgation of the Nuremberg Laws, we found out that Inge was a "half-Jew." The mounting*

tensions in society were reflected in our classroom, where there were sharp differences of opinion regarding politics.

Although I had sat next to Inge for quite some time, I was suddenly told to move to another seat and avoid any contact with her in the schoolyard. Since the order made no sense to me, I refused to comply with it.

Dorle Z. was the only one of us who joined the Resistance. She was released from prison in Bayreuth by the U.S. Army.

Many years later I was again made painfully aware of the Resistance. In June 1990 I received an invitation to the University of Geneva. Professor Cornelia Niebler-Gaedtke and the students in her translation class were studying whether women's autobiographies were significantly different from those written by men.

After reading my book, the students decided to invite me to their class. They had drawn up a long list of questions. One in particular touched me deeply. A student quoted a passage from my book in which I described my reaction to being barred from accepting a traineeship with a newspaper because I was a "half-breed":

I . . . walked across Rathausplatz, which had already been renamed in honor of Germany's great Leader. What pleasure could I take in the splendid neoclassical arcades beside the Kleine Alster—what pleasure could I take in the whole of this lovely, beloved city— if the sense of belonging was denied me. . . . With mingled sentimentality and earnestness, I wondered what life had left to offer me. But I never asked myself

*that question again. . . . I never wished to be anyone
or anything else—not even "Aryan."*

"That just about bowled me over," said the young language student. "How could a young person cope like that?"

It is not easy when you are suddenly asked a question
that you had never thought about before.

"I don't really know. But I'm glad I *did.* I knew enough
companions in misfortune who would have preferred to be
someone else, who just couldn't take being ostracized."

I told the students that my next book would deal with
just such conflicts. Most of all, I thought of my own
brother, who would so much have liked to play soccer for
the Hamburg Athletic Club. And I thought of the many
others who until recently were unable to discuss the past
and could do so now only because there are people in
Germany who are genuinely interested in their stories.
And I thought of those who are still unable to talk about
what they had gone through.

In this respect I had it easier.

In the evening we went to see Michael Verhoeven's and
Mario Krebs's film *Die Weisse Rose* (*The White Rose*). The
following day I phoned Little Inge and asked, "How come
we didn't know about those horrific death sentences at that
time?"

"Because at that time, our friends and relatives in
Hamburg were being rounded up every day to be deported.
Because bombs were continually being dropped on the city.
And because we were moving to a country retreat in Staufen."

And also because those in our group who were in contact with the Munich students were pledged to silence—
even we were kept in the dark about their activities.

That evening in Geneva, I read a detailed account of the

student resistance network at the University of Munich in Inge Scholl's book.[8]

There is one time I will never forget. I was invited to give a reading at Frau Dörte Hell-Rubow's bookshop in Fuhlsbüttel. She had arranged the inside of the store so as to create a friendly atmosphere, placing me at the center of a rather large audience. Directly across from me sat a well-groomed elderly lady who kept eyeing me intently.

After I finished my reading and put down my book, there was a prolonged silence. Then the elderly lady began to ask questions that indicated just how well informed she was. She inquired in particular about my mother, my brother, and then all of a sudden about my cousin.

"Did you know my family in the old days?" I asked.

"In 1926," she said as her voice began to break, "I worked as a typist in your father's law office."

There was a deathly silence. It seemed as though the entire audience shared in this emotional encounter. Frau Paul N. began to talk about those years. She told how she had typed the commemorative publication that my father had compiled to celebrate the anniversary of his lodge.

"I asked him, 'How do you spell "Shakespeare," and who is he?' The next day Dr. Hecht gave me two tickets to the theater to see a Shakespeare play. That's the kind of person he was."

And that's the way it was.

I had never heard of this commemorative publication before. Frau N. had sent her copy to her children in America. She later got it back and wrote me on July 23:

> [T]he book is finally back in my hands again, and I'll make sure you receive it soon. . . . I got to know your

parents in those days. . . . They were kind enough to take me to the theater for a gala performance of Nathan der Weise. *So much for those days. I am now about to turn eighty. . . . Old wounds are opening up again. People didn't know anything or want to know anything, because they weren't directly affected. It's all so sad. Life treated you so cruelly. . . . And we stuck our heads in the sand. What could we do? I could tell you lots of stories about the time I worked for your father's firm. If you lived in Hamburg, we could exchange many of our innermost thoughts. I enjoyed reading your book. You describe everything so accurately and concisely. . . . I will never forget it.*

NOTES

1. Simha Naor, *Krankengymnastin in Auschwitz. Aufzeichnungen des Häftlingss Nr. 80574* (Freiburg: Herder-Verlag, 1986).

2. "Next to Günter Grass and Martin Walser, Siegfried Lenz is the most highly acclaimed and popular living German novelist and author of short stories; along with Grass, Walser, and Heinrich Böll, he has helped to shape the path of German literature since 1951. . . . Since 1951 he has lived in Hamburg." Hans Wagener, "Siegfried Lenz (1926–)," in *Contemporary German Fiction Writers*, 2d ser., edited by Wolfgang D. Elfe and James Hardin (Ann Arbor, Mich.: Gale Research Co., 1988), 182.—TRANS.

3. Mrs. F. is referring to my account of my school days. The clergyman who gave us religious instruction suddenly began to ignore me.

4. It was these brutal events, unnoticed by most people (including myself), that caused the young Jew Herschel Grynszpan, whose parents had themselves been expelled from Germany, to assassinate a Nazi diplomat in Paris on November 8, 1938. It was a murder that had grave consequences for the Jews remaining in Germany.

5. Barbara Gehrts, *Nie wieder ein Wort davon?* (Munich: Deutscher Taschenbuch-verlag, 1978, 1984). [*Don't Say a Word*, trans. Elizabeth D. Crawford (New York: M. K. McElderry Books, 1986).—TRANS.]

6. Antje Dertinger, *Weisse Möwe—Gelber Stern: das kurze Leben der Helga Beyer* (Bonn: H. W. Dietz Nachf., 1987).

7. Helge Grabitz, *NS-Prozesse: Psychogramme der Beteiligten* (Heidelberg: C. F. Müller, Juristischer Verlag, 1985).

8. Inge Scholl, *Die Weisse Rose* (Frankfurt am Main: Fischer Taschenbuchverlag, 1989). [*Six against Tyranny* (London: Murray, 1955).—TRANS.]

HOW OTHERS FARED

LIKE ME, MANY of my readers were unable to forget the past, and for that reason they often wrote to me. Now I'd like to give some of them a chance to tell their stories in their own words. It was from reading their stories, by the way, that I myself learned just how many people had once inhabited that strange twilight zone between two worlds.

During one of my readings, I got to know Michael H. and later received the following letter from his mother:

TOSCA SCH.—DAUGHTER OF A "MIXED MARRIAGE"

Heiligenhafen, January 4, 1988
. . . When I read your book, I felt as if you were telling my story.
. . . Like you, I was born in Dr. Callmann's private clinic in Hamburg. My father was Jewish, my mother Christian. They lived in what was later called a "privileged mixed marriage." That heralded the beginning of an ordeal that was all too familiar in the Third Reich. I was barred from pursuing a university education or attending a government-sponsored commercial school. After giving birth to my first daughter in 1942, I was

*prohibited from marrying my fiancé. And when I became preg-
nant with my second child, I was threatened with internment in
a concentration camp if I dared to continue seeing the man to
whom I was engaged. I don't wish to describe the other forms of
persecution to which my family was subjected. . . .*

After marrying in 1948, Frau Sch. gave birth to two
sons. One of them was the aforementioned Michael. He
often writes me and asks for my help in locating information about his family, information that his mother is no
longer likely to have in her possession.

*This question involves the marriage of my mother's parents. I
approached her very cautiously about the matter, but she is still
quite sensitive when it comes to discussing her family background
or the Holocaust.*

Michael H. asked me about Nazi "arithmetic," that is,
the various degrees into which the children of "mixed marriages" were divided and the importance of a Jewish versus
a Christian marriage. Above all, he wanted to know where
he could obtain information on the subject. Fortunately for
those who are unable to deal with the complexities of the
laws directed against the Jews and "half-breeds," there is a
large body of literature on Nazi racial policy. And the
Landeszentralen für politische Bildung (Regional Centers
for Political Education) can also be of help in this regard.

WORKING WITHOUT A "CERTIFICATE
OF ARYAN ANCESTRY"

My friend Ursula in Haverstown wrote me quite a bit
about "mixed marriages":

What was particularly sad about some of them was the hostility that existed between family members who professed different faiths. My mother was married during the Great War, in 1914. My father was "Aryan." She was baptized a Protestant with her parents' consent. We children, that is, my brother Peter and I, were also baptized Protestant. We were a happy family until 1933.

Uncle Fritz, my mother's brother, married an Orthodox Jew. She was attractive, charming, and witty, and we all liked her. But as conditions in Germany worsened, her attitude changed, with grave consequences for us all. When the time came to get Grandfather out of the country, she made sure that his faithful housekeeper would accompany him. Because she was "Aryan," his housekeeper was in no particular danger, of course, and had no urgent need to leave Germany. My mother, on the other hand, was in an increasingly precarious situation and would very much have liked to accompany Grandfather abroad and take her "half-Aryan" daughter along with her. . . .

After we began making preparations to emigrate, I decided to become a nurse. As a nurse, one could survive anywhere. However, no hospital would accept me as a trainee, not even the Jewish hospital. Understandably, Jewish nurse trainees were preferred, since they were in the most immediate danger.

We were always falling between two stools. . . . I remember how we loved to go to the movies and see Broadway musicals—until they were banned when the war broke out. Ever since I was a little girl, I had wanted to be a dancer, especially a tap dancer. So in the morning I took classes at the Sauer School (to which I had the good fortune of being admitted) and in the afternoons I baby-sat. After I became proficient in tap dancing, I was supposed to perform with the school dance company at the Flora Music Hall. In order do so, I would have had to enroll in the school's Department of Performing Arts; however, I was barred from

187

applying. So Frau Sauer allowed me to dance on the Reeperbahn, where no one asked me to show "proof of Aryan ancestry." [1] *Frau Sauer advised me always to mention the fact that my brother was in the Wehrmacht. His birth year, 1916, was still subject to conscription. Frau Sauer, by the way, always treated me very humanely. When I didn't have enough money to pay my school fees, she never pressed me. And sometimes she would allow me to defray the cost of my tuition by helping her sew costumes.*

It is quite difficult to imagine our gentle and proper friend Ursula dancing on the Reeperbahn. But at least she had some fun, and those times did do her a world of good. Nonetheless, she had many painful experiences in Hamburg. I'd like to relate in Ursula's own words the following "funny" story—if one may use that word in this context—that unfolded after she returned from a trip to Copenhagen. She had gone to the Danish capital to contact the lodge brothers of a Hamburg Freemason and inform them about his desperate situation:

A short time later, after the war began, I received a summons to appear early in the morning at Gestapo headquarters in City Hall. No reason was given. With her lively imagination, my mother could already see me being arrested as a spy. Thank goodness I was naive and didn't worry a lot. When I said goodbye to her at 7:15 A.M., Mother replied: "I'm going to pull the covers over my head and won't get out of bed until you're back."

I didn't have long to wait before I was directed to a Gestapo official. First, he asked to see my ID card. Then he inquired, "Are you half-Aryan?"
"Yes."
"Do you live with your mother?"
"Yes."

"Do you have a radio?"

"Yes."

*"Are you aware that your mother is not allowed to listen to the radio?"*²

"Yes."

"So where do you *listen to the radio?"*

"On the toilet."

At 10:30 A.M. I got Mummy out of bed. We drank coffee together and—if I recall correctly—after we began to relax and feel relieved, we laughed ourselves silly.

Although I usually refrain from giving my own interpretation of stories that speak for themselves, I feel obliged to point out that the officials at Gestapo headquarters were grown men, after all, and would have been perfectly aware that Ursula's brother Peter was serving in the army at that time. Nevertheless, I still admire her presence of mind.

In Shanghai

Like Nanking, this Chinese city on the Huangpu had been attacked and occupied by the Japanese in 1937. Under certain conditions, Jews from Germany were permitted to immigrate to Shanghai; this was often their last avenue of escape. Since they had been stripped of their German citizenship by the Nazis, they were considered stateless. In my book, I described the circumstances in which my uncle Edgar and his family lived in Shanghai after being forced to emigrate from Hamburg.

Ursula and her mother also ended up in Shanghai. Their situation was exceptional in that Frau G.'s passport had been stamped with that infamous capital *J*.³ So she was not

189

permitted to leave the ghetto that the Japanese—as Germany's allies—had established in the city. Ursula, however, was allowed "to breathe the air of freedom," a phrase that, as will become clear in the following quotation, she meant to be taken quite literally:

> *Given the limits that had been set on what I was permitted to learn at school in Hamburg, the fact that I had taken private Danish lessons turned out to be of even greater benefit than I could ever have imagined. In Shanghai I quickly found a job working for a Danish family with two small children. Luckily I still had a German passport that wasn't stamped with a J. So when "my" family traveled to Tsingtao in the summer to vacation at the seashore, the Japanese issued me a visa; otherwise, I wouldn't have been able to accompany them. In Tsingtao, a French family soon attracted my attention. Word spread quickly that they were Vichy loyalists.[4] Whenever I happened to be in their presence, they made all sorts of nasty remarks. Though I had made it a point to speak nothing but Danish, they must have found out that I was a German refugee.*
>
> *After I had been in Shanghai for two and a half years, I heard about a German family that was seeking to hire a nanny. The wife was a native of Hamburg married to an Italian who had been transferred to Hong Kong as an agent for Lloyd Triestino. When the political situation in the Far East began to deteriorate, he sent his family to Shanghai and was subsequently interned by the British. The German consulate then became responsible for supporting his family. Soon afterward, a letter arrived from a con-*

sular official warning them that if they did not dis-
miss their "half-Aryan" nanny at once (I had been
working for them for just six months), they would no
longer receive a subsistence allowance.

Ursula was hired by another German family. However, her passport, which had to be renewed periodically, was a constant source of concern.

In order to renew it, I had to go to the German con-
sulate. I did not particularly look forward to those vis-
its. In fact, the only time I felt good about them was
after I had got what I had come for and could go home
with a renewed passport in hand. After all, whenever I
was in that building I was de jure on German soil—
and I had no idea what might be going through the
minds of the officials there. I was generally treated in a
patronizing manner. You have to remember that a
valid passport was a matter of life and death. Then,
under Nazi pressure, the Japanese established a ghetto
for stateless refugees in part of the Hongkew section of
Shanghai. At first only mothers were relocated there. I
moved to Hongkew only after I married my husband,
Herbert, who was already living in the ghetto.
The ghetto had no trees or bushes or decent places
for children to play. I remember in particular a fam-
ily with two little blond children. They were so pale,
it seemed that besides being malnourished, they were
growing up without any exposure to sunlight or fresh
air. Though I myself managed quite nicely, I was
unable to help—it was a very painful feeling.
Before war broke out between Japan and the
United States, Mother tried her best to find some

way of immigrating to America. However, there were now additional obstacles to overcome: Peter had been in the Wehrmacht. It seemed we were always on the wrong side.

Then one day the Germans refused to renew Ursula's passport. Fortunately for her, though, she was not forced to surrender the expired document.

I still went out, of course. What else should have I have done? I relied on the fact that the Japanese who manned the checkpoints could not read German. A passport with a swastika on it, my photograph in it, and a few official stamps was sufficient identification for them to allow me to move freely around Shanghai. . . . If I had not been forced to remain helpless in the face of all the misery in Hongkew, my life as an expatriate would have been one long adventure. But Mummy was suffering from malnutrition caused by diarrhea, and Herbert had painful sores on his feet. It was Herbert who saved my mother from starving to death. When we entered the United States, she weighed all of ninety pounds—and she was not exactly a petite woman.

My employers had bought a little summer house outside Shanghai where we would spend the oppressively hot summers. What I wouldn't have given to be able to take the children of Hongkew there and watch them blossom in the fresh air and eat healthful food— but it was simply out of the question . . . !

Fortunately, there was one time, however, when Ursula was not on the "wrong" side:

When U.S. bombers raided Hongkew on July 17, 1945, I had the good fortune to be on the "right" side. When we heard American planes flying overhead, we looked up at the sky and felt happy that the Yanks were coming. But then the bombs started falling; they inflicted serious injuries on us refugees. Didn't the Americans realize we were their friends? The Japanese had cleverly placed the ghetto inside their industrial zone in China! The building I was in took a direct hit; eight people were killed. Although I had a couple of broken ribs and a number of cuts due to flying glass, I managed to crawl out from under the rubble on my own power and get to a first-aid station. . . .

This was the same raid in which my jolly uncle Edgar was killed. I told his story in my book.

As I mentioned earlier, Ursula's brother Peter served in the Wehrmacht. However, as a "half-breed," he was automatically declared "unfit for military service" after the so-called Rust decree was issued on July 2, 1942.[5] He then became a forced laborer and was shipped to France. When the war ended in the West, he had quite a time explaining his status to the victorious Allies. Almost all the "half-breeds" who had been inducted into the German armed forces were in a similar predicament. My brother, who was born in 1923, was spared the humiliation of being drafted into the Wehrmacht and then being unceremoniously booted out.

Peter lives in Canada. When I asked him to write his own story, he replied in the negative. He was neither willing nor able to talk about his experiences.

THE FLIGHT OF HERMANN LANGE, OR *"NE NADO"*

Hermann Lange found himself in the same situation as Peter after the war. He now lives in Munich and studies, among other things, the history and fate of the "half-breeds." Unlike Peter, he was both willing and able to describe his "schizophrenic" existence. His account begins when the war was nearly over and he found himself between the front lines of two armies.

With the aid of a bicycle I had "borrowed" from the OT⁶ office, I made good my escape from the forced labor camp. The OT had been ordered by the Gestapo to guard and supervise us. It was Sunday, April 15, 1945, and I was then some thirty kilometers east of Leipzig, hoping to be liberated by the advancing Americans. How could I have known that Eisenhower would decide to halt his forces at the Elbe and Mulde Rivers?

So I developed a new strategy. If the Americans wouldn't come to me, I would go to them. West of the Mulde, I headed north. On a dirt road just outside the village of Raguhn, I was stopped by a lieutenant in the artillery. Having just been shot down from a linden tree—his observation post—he was pretty ticked off. Since I was twenty-four at the time, I looked like a deserter. Given the fact that the enemy had already taken the nearest village, the officer didn't buy my story about working for the OT and being on my way to OT headquarters in Berlin. He marched me off to division headquarters, where I was interrogated by the IC, the officer in charge of counterintelligence and espionage. It was amazing how well the military apparatus still functioned in spite of everything! Finally, this general staff type declared himself uninterested in anybody working for the OT and ordered me to leave. "And by the way, if you're going to Berlin, you're headed in the wrong direction."

While I was in the woods east of the Mulde, I reconsidered my situation. The main line of resistance wasn't a particularly safe area for a semi-illegal. Nevertheless, if I remained in hiding, I could hold out until the Americans arrived. If things became too uncomfortable or too bellicose or the weather got too cold, I always had the option of trying to make a run for Berlin. What I couldn't possibly know in the isolation of my forest glade was that the Soviets had launched a major offensive along the Oder; it was the beginning of the battle for Berlin. For three days and four nights I camped out on Düben Heath. Thank goodness the weather was clement: no April showers, and the nights were mild. I had sufficient K rations to tide me over. From time to time I would take short walks. Once I got so thirsty, I dared to enter a forester's lodge—and I even took time to shave.

Friday, April 20. There wasn't a Yank in sight or within earshot. I pumped up the tires of my bicycle, hopped on, and pedaled hard. It was a glorious spring day: the fruit trees were in bloom along the road; the countryside was peaceful. I dreamed of vacation trips, open borders, and Lydia the Slovak girl. But appearances were deceiving. The defensive front in the East was collapsing. Russian artillery was lobbing shells into Berlin. Hitler appeared in public for the last time, on the day of his fifty-sixth birthday.

My problem was getting across the Elbe unscathed.

The Wehrmacht had detachments of officers scouring the countryside in search of deserters. I learned to be very wary. As the place to make my crossing I chose Pretzsch, a little-known little village situated between the towns of Wittenberg and Torgau. Just five days later, Russian and American soldiers would shake hands at Torgau. On the Elbe ferry out of Pretzsch, I was promptly nabbed by an officers' patrol. It was no use arguing with them; they needed every man they could lay their hands on. Luftwaffe men from the south, sailors from the north—everyone had to pass this point on their way home. They figured as an OT man I knew how to blow up bridges. A spirited sergeant received me as a welcome addition to his recently established company. Later I learned that this was all part of the process of raising the new Twelfth Army—the often-mentioned Wenck Army on which Hitler had pinned his last hopes. The sergeant major sent me to get a new set of clothes. Just as I was coming to terms with my new status, a reserve lieutenant, seated comfortably in a corner, asked me to tell my story all over again, which by that time I could rattle off without skipping a beat. He nodded sympathetically and had orders issued for me to go to Berlin, something I had never dared to hope would happen. Now I'm legal! Nobody can stop me or do anything else to me anymore, I thought. That same evening I left the town of Pretzsch.

I vanished into the night and struggled down a bumpy country road until I reached the village of Jessen. A farmer's wife—a raw-boned, medium-size woman—allowed me to sleep in her empty stable. As she handed me a piece of bread, she suddenly said, "It's *the Jews who are to blame for the war." I was dumb-founded. It's hard to believe, but throughout the entire Nazi period I had never experienced any anti-Semitism on a personal level (except for the bureaucratic variety), and then this, on the eve of the thousand-year Reich's collapse!*

Barely two hours later, the village siren sounded. Tank alert! The Russians were coming. I set off at once, leaving a five-mark bill behind; I didn't want to accept any gifts from that woman. A column of automobiles was coming toward me, raising huge clouds of dust—one official Mercedes after another, absolutely packed, each one the property of some government ministry or party office, the heads of which were all fleeing south that night. I crossed the military training grounds at Jüterbog, where I had taken part in maneuvers as a communications specialist back in '39, that is, when I was still "permitted" to do so. A year later, Hitler ordered members of this undesirable mongrel race to be barred from serving in the armed forces. My former buddies ended up staying permanently in Stalingrad. The night was clear and unusually quiet. There wasn't the slightest trace of a German soldier. I had to circle the spearhead of a Russian armored column. A little farther to the east, it turned out, the German Ninth Army was in the process of being surrounded. After trekking sixty kilometers across the sands of the Brandenburg March, luckily with the wind to my back, I arrived at my destination—Woltersdorf, a village five kilometers north of Luckenwalde—around ten in the morning.

A train, its locomotive belching steam, was about to depart Woltersdorf station. It was the last train to

Berlin. In a flash I considered my options. The train would take me home to my family, but what if I happened to end up in the final stages of the battle of Berlin? Here, on the other hand, it looked as if a "change of program," as it were, was imminent and would take place quickly.

Sunday, April 22, was to be a dramatic day. The Soviets entered the suburbs of Berlin. Hitler suffered a nervous breakdown, claiming that the war was lost and everyone had betrayed him.

Throughout the day, the tanks of Konev's Fourth Guards Tank Army rolled toward Potsdam. In three days the ring around Berlin would be closed.

The inside of the building was searched from top to bottom. A hulking Soviet soldier then went on to scour every nook and cranny in the basement.

He came across parts of a hidden uniform and frisked his "civilian" captive, finding a photo of him in a Wehrmacht uniform.

I was dragged out of the building and plopped down on a garden chair. I felt a gun at the back of my neck. However, it seemed that the weapon wasn't working properly. I turned my head and saw the Russian soldier fiddling with the barrel.

I simply had to speak to an officer. Hearing my cries, a lieutenant came over and asked the standard "Kto eto?"—"Who's this?"

"I'm from the camp," I replied. Luckily, I knew enough Russian to get by. From the seam of my jacket I removed documentation to verify my identity: a scrap of paper on which a friend of mine from the

camp, a Russian POW named Dimitri K., had attest-
ed to my reliability; a passport-size photo of me taken
by the Gestapo, a kind of mug shot with the registra-
tion number 3411 written in large numerals. The
photo had the desired effect. The lieutenant ordered my
tormentor: "Ne nado"—"There's no need to shoot
him." I'll never forget those two Russian words.

I must have blacked out. When I came to, I was
being marched down a village road in the middle of a
group of German POWs. I was paraded past a staff
officer, a well-built man in a spotless uniform who
spoke fluent German. He understood my situation
and even gave me some well-intentioned advice,
namely that I should claim to be a Jew. No Russian
soldier was going to understand such subtle Fascist
distinctions as "half-Jew" or "quarter-Jew." As a
Jew, I wouldn't be viewed as a German, and I would
be left alone, because Jews, he said, were a separate
nationality in the Soviet Union. With that, he
released me.

Herr Lange also described the frightening days during
which Russian soldiers hunted for alcohol and women:

During the night of April 30 to May 1, the alert
sounded. Soviet multiple rocket launchers howled.
Nearby, what was left of the German Ninth Army
was fighting its way west. Naturally, we were appre-
hensive about the upcoming Russian May Day cele-
brations. We were pleasantly surprised, however.
Soviet soldiers regaled us with bread, sardines in oil,
and vodka. We celebrated together in the garden. The
sun shone. And we heard that Hitler had shot himself.

The last chapter of my bizarre journey began on Thursday, May 3, 1945. The capital of the Reich had surrendered. I was very concerned about my relatives who were still living there. I thought I could get a pass—propusk in Russian—to go to Berlin. At Soviet military headquarters in Luckenwalde I gave my spiel, stressing the fact, as I had just been instructed, that I was a Jew. The reaction of the commissar or whatever he was surprised me: "Jews in our country have to serve." He used the word sluzhit'; I hadn't heard wrong. As you know, it's not exactly proper to protest in such circumstances. The first act I had to perform in the line of duty was to sweep the courtyard clean.

Outside, the pride of the Soviet army rolled past: an armada of T-34 tanks overloaded with men, women, gasoline canisters, arms, and every imaginable type of equipment. It was an awesome spectacle as the tanks roared and rumbled by; the streets and buildings shook. At the headquarters of the Soviet military, liberated American POWs celebrated when they saw their fellow countrymen again—U.S. Army reporters on an excursion to Berlin.

The next morning I was handed a rifle, a Mauser 98k, and shown how to use it. My instruction in arms lasted less than five minutes. I was assigned to an escort patrol convoying German POWs. From Luckenwalde we marched south down a dusty road. I thought about the various roles I had played during the past three weeks: a laborer in the custody of the Gestapo; a fugitive with inadequate identification drafted as a sapper, taken prisoner, and almost executed as a tank gunner; and now a kind of collaborator attached to the Soviet army. I felt anything but comfortable in the latter role, which was to be of only short duration. At first I placed myself at the tail end of the marching column so it wouldn't appear as if I were guarding German soldiers. A liberated Pole marched beside me. Like me, he was in civilian dress, but being in a playful mood, he had put on a Nazi storm trooper's brown service cap.

In Jüterbog a change of escort took place. While it was going on, I attracted the attention of the Russian commander of the guard. He decided that I wasn't a Russian Jew, but a German civilian prisoner. What prompted him to make that determination was the fact that when I was asked the question "Where were you born?" I responded truthfully by saying Berlin, and not, for example, Minsk. I was relieved of my rifle as quickly as I had acquired it. My countrymen were surprised when they saw their new fellow prisoner. We continued our trek, and after a day's march of forty kilometers, we spent the night in a barn just outside the town of Dahme.

Although I felt relieved that I was no longer in the Red Army, I didn't particularly take to my new status. If I don't get out of here soon, I thought, I'll end up somewhere in the Soviet Far East. We got nothing to eat; fights erupted among the exhausted enlisted men over every scrap of bread that the women along the road handed us. We came upon a farm around noon and went hog wild. Two Russian sentries guarded the front gate. However, whenever a chicken cackled, the sentries would immediately

201

*chase it down. That was my chance, and I used it to
slip through the gate. Outside on the village green I
was surrounded by a host of Russian soldiers.* "Voina
kaput" *("The war's over") and* "Ty domoi" *("You
can go home"), they shouted at me. Evidently, I was
free, so I scurried off.*

*The rest of the story can be told quite quickly. By the
evening of May 6, I was back in Woltersdorf. I had
struggled along dirt roads and down forest paths, sat-
isfying my hunger with a tin of mixed vegetables,
eaten cold and unsalted. On May 8, news of
Germany's surrender arrived. I heard Churchill's
great speech on the radio. When he ended with "Long
live the cause of freedom," I must confess that it
moved me deeply. The next day I was back on my OT
bicycle, this time headed for home.*

*Our house on Gräfenbergweg was still standing.
During the fighting it had been used as the command
post for a Soviet battalion. On one of those days, a
young Russian lieutenant got my mother out of the
basement and took her over to the globe that stood in
my room. First he pointed to the huge area covered by
the Soviet Union, then to the tiny little German
Reich, and in a mixture of German and Russian said,*
"Gitler ferikt!"—"Hitler crazy!"

NOTES

1. The Reeperbahn is a sleazy strip of clip joints, sex shows,
and wholesale prostitution in the notorious Hamburg sub-
urb of St. Pauli.—TRANS.

2. After the war began, Jews (and many others besides) were forced to surrender their radios.

3. On October 5, 1938, the Reich Ministry of the Interior published a decree ordering every Jew of German or Austrian nationality to hand in his or her passport so that it could be stamped with a capital *J* (for *Jude*, or "Jew") to single out Jews and bar them from entering another country.—TRANS.

4. Vichy is a spa town in central France, the name of which became associated with the French government under Marshal Pétain that collaborated with Nazi Germany from 1940 to 1944. The Vichy government even went so far as to hand over Jewish refugees in the unoccupied zone to the Nazi police.

5. Bernhard Rust (1883–1945) was a Nazi politician and Reich minister for science, education, and public instruction.—TRANS.

6. Organisation Todt (Todt Organization) was a semicivilian state construction organization that built important military facilities, e.g., the so-called Westwall, the fortress line along Germany's western frontier.

ENCOUNTERS AND THEIR BENEFICIAL EFFECTS

IT HAS BECOME customary in Germany to invite émigrés to visit their former hometowns, a practice I first learned about in an article that appeared in *Die Welt* on May 10, 1984:

> **Visitors Rediscover Past—Harbor No Ill Feelings**
> *It is comforting to know that the words inscribed over the entrance to the Rathaus once again ring true. "The freedom won by our forefathers repays the efforts made by our posterity to preserve it," wrote Siegfried Tand from London, paraphrasing the Latin original to express his gratitude for having been invited to visit his native Hamburg.[1] Yesterday was the seventh time that former Jewish citizens of this city were received in the Kaisersaal of the Rathaus and regaled with a breakfast hosted by the city Senate. . . . On this occasion there were thirty guests—from Britain, the United States,*

and Israel. . . . For Goldie Abt, Hamburg was just the
first stop during her trip to Germany. After her stay
in the city on the Elbe, she will be picked up by her
daughter who resides in Freiburg.

Like all other such guests of the city of Hamburg, Frau
Abt was presented with a copy of *Invisible Walls*—a practice
that I naturally found flattering. Fortunately for both of us,
she learned from my book that I too lived in Freiburg,
where her daughter Roslyn, a professor at Wayne State
University in Detroit, had come in August 1983 to study
for a year at the university. Roslyn was accompanied by her
husband, Professor Marvin Schindler, who also taught at
Wayne State. In addition to his teaching responsibilities, he
headed the school's Junior Year in Germany office and was
in charge of the Junior Year in Freiburg Program for the
academic year 1983–84.

The main focus of Roslyn's research is postwar German
literature dealing with the Holocaust. She therefore found
my book an important resource. After she read it, we often
worked together. She is planning to write a paper about
Invisible Walls, tentatively titled "Historical Consciousness
and a Sense of (Re)Discovery."[2] In 1987 she published a
paper in which she discussed Lotte Paepcke's book *Ein
kleiner Händler, der mein Vater war*, the story of a Jewish
businessman and city councilman in Freiburg.[3] And in 1990
she published another paper under the title "The Writings
of Ralph Giordano and Ingeborg Hecht: Toward a New
Enlightenment."[4]

The first time I attended one of the breakfasts hosted by
the Hamburg Senate in the city's lovely Rathaus was in

206

August 1984. The Rathaus had been officially dedicated in 1897 and was graced with the motto referred to earlier. After 1933 its words, inscribed in golden letters, no longer reflected the reality of life in the city. Many individuals of Jewish origin had helped build the city of Hamburg, yet for twelve long years nobody made any effort to preserve *their* freedom.

Now, however, the city was doing its best to make amends.

At lunch Little Inge and I had many emotional encounters. Naturally, a number of names came up that were associated with Hamburg; people inquired about old friends and acquaintances. They learned many painful things, but also many things that brought them closer together. There were guests present who had known my parents, and we relived a number of experiences together.

Among the visitors were Esther and Ernst Mayer, a married couple from Haifa. Ernst had taught at the Talmud-Torah School, and Esther came from a Freiburg family. I met both of them again a week later, because Freiburg, in the same friendly spirit as Hamburg, also sponsored homecomings for its former Jewish citizens. A slight digression: On April 10, 1989, the NDR television network broadcast a moving documentary directed by Renate Zilligen: *Ein Ort, den ich verlassen musste—Jüdisches Leben am Grindel (A Place I Was Forced to Leave—Jewish Life in Grindel)*. In the film I again saw Ernst talking about his life in Hamburg. One particular shot, however, had to do with my life as well. "I thought of you when I was shooting it. You'll see what I mean," Frau Zilligen told me. When I did see the film, I was deeply touched. The camera focused in on a little wine bar in Grindelallee that plays a sad and macabre part in *Invisible Walls*. The song used as background music also reminded me of that scene in the restaurant with the two SS men: "O my hometown, your stars. . . ."

At the Rathaus get-together I also got to know Ursula Randt, who had written a history of the Jewish girls' school on Karolinenstrasse.[5] Her book evoked memories for which many people are deeply grateful. This important work was occasioned by a chance encounter that took place in 1972. "I am a special-education instructor for students with speech disabilities," she wrote in her introduction.

> *I worked at the school for more than six years and knew every nook and cranny in the building—from the basement to the attic. One day we were told to vacate it and move into a new modern building. In the middle of all the hustle and bustle, a little elderly lady was suddenly standing in front of me, speaking. I had never seen her before, and she didn't know me, either. She spoke with visible emotion. "Can you imagine," she said, "this is my old school. I attended it from 1909 to 1918. Did you know that this was once a Jewish girls' school?"*

It took just a few words for Frau Randt to learn of the terrible fate suffered by most of the students, a fate reflected in the year her history ends—1942. "I've been on every floor," said the elderly lady. "I was hoping to find something to show that this had once been our school, some token of remembrance. . . ."

It was after this encounter that Ursula Randt decided to write her book.

At the breakfast hosted by the Senate, one of the speakers urged the invited guests to write down their personal histories. Later, in 1989, I was presented with a copy of just such a book of recollections: *Fremd in der eigenen Stadt* (*A Stranger in My Own Town*).[6] It is the kind of book you flip through in search of familiar names. And I did in fact find one: Liese Rosenmeyer, "first-degree half-breed—no prospects."

Liese's husband, Thomas, the son of my great-uncle Kurt, appears in my book, where I told the story of his mother, whose fate was so closely intertwined with ours. What I learned by reading these reminiscences rounded out the picture of a young refugee woman who had fled to England only to find herself caught up in a bureaucratic mill at the beginning of the war—she was classified an "enemy alien."

Lieselotte, born in 1920, was the daughter of a Jewish doctor and his Christian wife. She raised her two daughters in her mother's faith.

> [W]hen I left school in 1937, I knew that as a "first-degree half-breed" I had no future in Germany. We were barred from entering an apprenticeship or any other kind of training program. I subsequently spent a year at a home economics school run by the Moravian Brothers at Königsfeld in the Black Forest. The kind and understanding Sister Peters never asked anyone to show proof of their racial acceptability. To this day I have the fondest memories of my year there. Many of the girls in the school came from outside Germany. . . . Since both I and the non-German

students were excluded from political indoctrination classes, we grew even closer to one another. In April 1938 I returned to my parents' home in Hamburg. . . . With each passing day the Nuremberg Laws made our lives more difficult. So I decided to accept an invitation from an English girlfriend of mine . . . to visit her in London. . . . It was around this time that my father was stripped of his physician's title and his nameplate was removed from the building in which he had his practice. Our daily lives became more and more burdensome and unpleasant. I wanted to be free and could see no future for us in Hitler's Germany. At that time I was a member of the Association of Non-Aryan Christians and met regularly with a number of like-minded young people who had similar feelings. On October 20, 1938, I sailed for England aboard the Hapag steamship Southampton. . . .

That was the last time I saw my parents for many years to come. I had a lovely vacation in England. The people—the whole atmosphere— seemed so free and so different from those I had known in Germany. After Chamberlain went to Munich, I was determined not to return home. I phoned my parents and told them I was going to stay in England to be trained as a nurse—one of the few professions open to me given my lack of funds. I was determined not to work as a domestic.

I persuaded my parents to send my little ten-year-old sister to me on the next Children's Transport.[7] I assured them that I would find her a family in England that would take her in. They reluctantly agreed. At that time I didn't understand my parents' hesitation. Only much later, when I had a ten-year-

old daughter of my own, did I realize how terribly hard the decision must have been for them.

Through a refugee organization known as Wobourne House, I found my sister a family to live with in London. One of the last children to get out of Germany in the spring of 1939, she arrived with just a small suitcase and a knapsack, her favorite teddy bear peeking out of one of the pockets. A lot of tears were shed. I was already in the first year of the nursing program at Wembley Hospital. Almost every day I would get a call from her asking if she couldn't return home to our parents. It was a difficult time for both of us; only gradually did she get over her homesickness.

The moment the war broke out, the hospital abruptly dismissed all their refugee employees; we were informed that we were "enemy aliens." We couldn't understand how anybody could do such a thing to us. Special tribunals were established to divide all Germans and Austrians residing in Great Britain into three categories. Those placed in Category A were judged hostile and were to be interned immediately. I was classified in Category C, no threat to national security. After the British evacuation from Dunkirk in the spring of 1940, almost all male refugees in the three categories were interned on the Isle of Man, and many of them were later shipped to Canada or Australia. My husband, Thomas Rosenmeyer from Hamburg, was one of those who was deported to Canada. Nurses like myself were put up in large private homes and given a small allowance by the Committee on Refugees. Our fate was argued in Parliament; the question being debated by the MPs was whether there were spies in our ranks.

When Lieselotte finally completed her education, she was awarded a gold medal for being the best in her class. She commented, "At last some acknowledgement. Later I trained . . . to become a midwife, a profession that I greatly enjoyed."

Lieselotte described how elated she was when—all too rarely—she received a message through the Red Cross, limited to no more than twenty-five words, indicating that her parents were still alive. What she wrote next brings us back again to my book: "In the terrible night bombing raid of 1944, my parents lost everything they owned. A good friend and former patient of my father, Elisabeth Flügge, gave my parents shelter in her home and then allowed them to live with her until the end of the war." That same Frau Flügge had once been my teacher; in my book I wrote about her courageous actions and the currant that had been planted in her honor on the Avenue of the Righteous at Yad Vashem to recognize the help she had given to so many people.

FINDING EACH OTHER AGAIN

In February 1985 a letter from out of the distant past reached me at my Freiburg address.

Dear Ingeborg,
I don't know if I'm still allowed to call you by your first name. In the old days you used to call me Evchen, but that was a long time ago. I'll begin at the beginning. One day as I was browsing through some bookstores in Hamburg, I saw your book Invisible Walls. *I instantly recognized the photograph on the jacket; it was that beautiful house on Frauenthal where my mother and I used to be invited for kaffeeklatsches when I was a young girl. I was so*

excited when I saw the book that I bought a copy to take home with me and read it through at one go. It evoked so many memories that I couldn't sleep a wink that night. But before I go on, let me introduce myself. My father was Dr. Adolf Calmann, the brother of your grandmother Hanna. You write that all of you were born in Dr. Calmann's clinic.

Oh, Evchen, you ask if you may still call me by my first name? If you only knew how happy I was to find another survivor of the time when we were children. . . . After Evchen entered my life again, all kinds of other memories began to surface. I especially recalled the first time my family suffered serious material hardships, when my father's practice was restricted and then shut down by government decree—hardships that our charitable relatives, the Calmanns, helped us time and again to overcome. Just a few years older than I, Evchen was my favorite cousin. I remember she had an electric-powered red "mini-carriage" to call her own! A "private car," as it were! How could anybody own something that was virtually unobtainable? I used to wonder. The most *we* could manage to get was a ride in a taxi when we had to be driven to the hospital to have our appendix removed or be treated for diphtheria. It was only when we were ill that we had the pleasure of riding in a car, which under the circumstances, of course, was anything but pleasurable.

"The things you do remember," said Evchen when I saw her again in Hamburg shortly after receiving her letter. "The things you do remember from over forty years ago. My parents never did let me drive that little contraption by myself. My big brother always had to go with me. It was awful!"

Everything is relative, Evchen. You have no idea how your "poor relations" adored that "little contraption."

213

Many letters reached me from out of the past—from schoolmates, neighbors, and others. But one letter from Essen, from an old people's home, made me particularly happy. It was from Emmi, our nanny; she was twenty-four when she left our service. I was now able to visit her and help celebrate her eightieth birthday.

"What I find most amazing," I said as I hugged her, "is that your voice sounds just like it did back then."

"Would you like to lecture here at the University of Hamburg?" Thomas Held asked me in the spring of 1985.

"Me—at the University of Hamburg?"

You have to remember that I hadn't been allowed to study anything, had never obtained a degree, and there I was, an "unskilled worker," as it were, being invited to give a "little lecture" in the Kokoschka Auditorium at the very heart of the ivory tower. The auditorium was close to Dillstrasse, where the "Jews' Houses" used to be. It was a strange sensation, but one that was also mixed with a sense of satisfaction.

The purpose of the evening's events was to memorialize Thomas's recently deceased professor, the sociologist Ernst W. Schepansky. Schepansky had assigned his students to do a study dealing with "foreigners, minorities, and outsiders." Our story—the story of the "half-breeds"—fitted in nicely with the focus of Schepansky's project.

After I finished giving my reading, the woman who was hosting the event, Professor M. E. Hille, encouraged the audience to begin a discussion. Finally, four gentlemen who were obviously too old to be students stood up and asked in unison: "How's your brother Wolfgang doing? We were classmates of his."

I'm sure that everyone in the audience sensed how

moving that moment was. What I didn't expect was that my encounter with the four gentlemen would ultimately stir someone else's emotions as well. In my book I described how strictly my brother had separated the past from the rest of his life. He lived in Central America, where German history wasn't exactly a hot topic. When his friends told me that they would very much like to invite him to visit, I knew that their invitation would touch him deeply but that he would probably decline. He was not in the best of health, and his business was not doing well, either. But then one day in April 1988, he decided to travel to Germany. Before leaving for Europe, he wrote to me to express his misgivings: "We really don't know each other anymore, my schoolmates and I." However, when we picked him up at the airport—when he saw his friends standing there, their faces beaming, holding beautiful bouquets—he suddenly regained his trust in people and never lost it again. It turned out to be an especially lovely week in Hamburg. The friends were all completely open with one another and didn't suppress their feelings. The self-consciousness that is often so difficult to overcome in such circumstances quickly evaporated. My brother's encounter with the past that week gave him a new attitude toward life.

"In coming here," said his friends, "he did more for us than he did for himself."

FRÄNZI—"HITLER COULD NOT TEAR THE
ROOTS OF FRIENDSHIP"

On December 2, 1938, our hiking companion and my classmate Fränzi left for England on a Children's Transport. She was seventeen. Her parents stayed behind—

and were deported. The last we heard about them was in a postcard we received from my father in Theresienstadt in which he wrote that Fränzi's parents had asked him to send their regards.

However, we were unable to pass on the news to Fränzi. The moment the war broke out, we lost contact with each other. When the war ended, we tried to find "our Fränzi" again. Since Inge and I no longer used our maiden names, she would have had great difficulty locating us.

In November 1978 I received a phone call; the person at the other end of the line sounded very excited: Little Inge had seen a television documentary about the Children's Transports.

"I recognized Fränzi."

NDR television was very helpful and sent Inge a still photograph of her. Again we tried to track Fränzi down, but with little success.

In the summer of 1988, Mrs. Ursula M. was reading *Invisible Walls* in Welwyn Garden City, England. She had discovered the book in a lending library. She had also been a classmate of mine, and once again we had found a "lost" friend.

Ursula knew where Fränzi lived—in the town of Merrick on Long Island.

We were overjoyed.

Fränzi wrote: "Our having found each other again is like recovering a precious part of my childhood."

In September, Inge flew to visit her in the States. Our story was written up in the local newspaper, the *Merrick Life*. Olga Drucker, a journalist who had also escaped from Germany on a Children's Transport, interviewed my two friends, both of whom now gazed at me from two photographs in the paper, one showing them at age seventeen and the other as they look today. The caption read: "Hitler could not tear the roots of friendship."

I had given Little Inge the postcard from Theresienstadt to take with her to America, since it really belongs to Fränzi.

Fränzi and her husband had vowed never to return to the country whose leaders had helped murder members of their family and rob them of their homeland. Their decision in May 1990 to go nevertheless represented an act of superhuman willpower. After arriving, they were determined to see their old friends again; however, I simply could not make myself get on a plane.

The same week in May during which they arrived, the Gedenk- und Bildungsstätte Israelitische Töchterschule (Jewish Girls' School Memorial Educational Foundation) on Karolinenstrasse was celebrating its first anniversary. The theme of the event was "Remembering for the Future," which is why I was invited to give a reading. It was a great personal honor for me because I had never attended the school myself, and the foundation had been established "in memory of former students and teachers who had lost their lives in the concentration camps." Both Fränzi and her husband were present on that May 28, even though they knew that my reading would revive some painful memories about our youth. But perhaps the very act of remembering had a cathartic effect.

MY ENCOUNTER WITH JOSEPH WALK

In March 1985—a year after my book was published—I received a letter that surprised and understandably delighted me. The letter came from Professor Joseph Walk in

Jerusalem. Walk had compiled a collection of documents regarding the legal status of Jews in Nazi Germany entitled *Das Sonderrecht für die Juden im NS-Staat (Anti-Jewish Legislation)*. It was his book that had inspired me in 1982 to write about the ways in which Nazi racial legislation had affected our lives during the Third Reich.[8] Professor Walk wrote as follows:

A teacher in Hamburg (an "Aryan" teacher) recently made me a gift of your book. I immediately read it from cover to cover, at one go. I scarcely need to tell you the great personal satisfaction I felt as a Jew, a human being, and an educator of many years' standing upon learning that it was my Sonderrecht *that prompted you to write* Invisible Walls! *When my book was released for publication (in 1981 in Bonn), people expressed a desire to personalize the dry legislative enactments by adding individual biographies, to show how these laws had affected the daily lives of "non-Aryans." As a small token of my appreciation, I am enclosing a photocopy of the address I delivered in Bonn in 1981.*

Dr. Jürgen Schmude was present when Dr. Walk's book was released, and he later wrote me the following with regard to Walk's compilation: "One must keep in mind the fate of those who were the object of this system [of laws] and its lethal consequences." It was precisely the burden of telling the story of the "half-breeds" while bearing in mind the often fatal consequences of the Nazis' racial legislation that proved so difficult—and still does. It was to the attainment of this goal that I directed my efforts.

In June 1990 Professor Walk came to Freiburg as part of a lecture tour of Germany. I therefore had the privilege of taking afternoon tea with the person whose painstaking scholarship had given me the initial inspiration for my book. That evening, in the packed auditorium of the Jewish Community Center, he reported on the efforts being undertaken by Israel to achieve peace in the Middle East.

NOTES

1. *Libertatem quam peperere maiores digne studeat servare posteritas.*—TRANS.

2. "Roslyn Schindler's paper 'Historical Consciousness and a Sense of (Re)Discovery' has not yet been published." E-mail from Roslyn Schindler (RSCHINDL@CMS.CC.WAYNE.EDU) to translator John Broadwin (BROADWIN@ADMIN.FHDA.EDU), 28 October 1997.—TRANS.

3. Lotte Paepcke, *Ein kleiner Händler, der mein Vater war* (Gütersloh: Gütersloher Verlagshaus Gerd Mohn, 1978). [Roslyn Schindler, "'Ohne Heimat': The Problem of Exile in the Works of Lotte Paepcke," in *Exile and Enlightenment, Festschrift for Guy Stern,* ed. Uwe Faulhaber, Jerry Glenn, Edward P. Harris, and Hans-Georg Richert (Detroit: Wayne State University Press, 1987), 131–39.—TRANS.]

4. Roslyn Schindler, "The Writings of Ralph Giordano and Ingeborg Hecht: Toward a New Enlightenment," in *The Enlightenment and Its Legacy, Studies in German Literature in Honor of Helga Slessarev,* ed. Sara Friedrichsmeyer and Barbara Becker-Cantarino (Bonn: Bouvier-Verlag, 1991), 195–207.—TRANS.

5. Ursula Randt, *Carolinenstrasse 35. Geschichte der Mädchenschule*

der Deutsch-Israelitischen Gemeinde in Hamburg, 1884–1942 (Hamburg: Selbstverlag Verein für Hamburgische Geschichte, 1984).

6. Charlotte Ueckert-Hilbert, ed., *Fremd in der eigenen Stadt. Erinnerungen jüdischer Emigranten aus Hamburg* (Hamburg: Junius-Verlag, 1989).

7. Children were sent to Britain under the auspices of the Movement for the Care of Children, briefly known as the Children's Transport.—Trans.

8. Joseph Walk, ed., *Das Sonderrecht für die Juden im NS-Staat: eine Sammlung der gesetzlichen Massnahmen und Richtlinien, Inhalt und Bedeutung* (Heidelberg, Karlsruhe: Müller Juristischer Verlag, 1981).

THE JOURNEY TO AMSTERDAM

THE ANNE FRANK RECOGNITION AWARD

ONE DAY IN JUNE 1985, I received a letter from Dr. Vincent C. Frank-Steiner in Basel: "Sincere congratulations." I read the enclosed press clipping with a mixture of surprise, disbelief, and joy.

> *The 1985 Anne Frank Prize for Literature has been awarded to Ida Fink for her book* A Scrap of Time, *published in German translation in 1983 by the Unionsverlag in Zurich. This is the first time that the Anne Frank Trust has awarded its literature prize for a work that truly reflects both the spirit and substance of* The Diary of Anne Frank. *The prizewinner was selected by a sixteen-member international committee. . . . .*
>
> *The Board of Trustees . . . has also decided . . . to honor the following authors with the Anne Frank*

Recognition Award: Klaus-Peter Wolf for Die Abschiebung, oder, Wer tötete Mahmut Perver? (The Deportation—or, Who Killed Mahmut Perver?), *Alexander Ramati for* The Assisi Underground, *and Ingeborg Hecht for* Invisible Walls. *The awards will be presented by the mayor of the city of Amsterdam on September 5, 1985.*

Given the fact that I hadn't emerged from my cubbyhole for more than thirty years and that my life had been confined mainly to the area around my apartment, I was quite literally bowled over by the news. I phoned Little Inge in Hamburg.

"OK," she said, "let's go to Amsterdam."

"Do you think I'll manage all right?"

"You have three months to get used to the idea," she calculated. That same day (the announcement of the award had already appeared in the newspaper) the congratulatory phone calls started coming in. A telegram from Dr. Hilde Claasen of my Hamburg publisher reminded me of the way my husband Hanns Studnicka greeted people, but then he had been an occasional employee of the same firm. My friend Ruth G. was ready to drive me to Amsterdam. Since she lives in the Hotzenwald, she needs a four-wheel-drive vehicle to get around.

"This time my Range Rover is going to be your home away from home," she said.

Apart from a class excursion to Copenhagen in the 1930s and some short trips to Alsace, this was my first journey abroad. For me, Amsterdam has always been the city of canals, bridges, and gabled housefronts—and of emigrants who often failed ultimately to escape the Nazis.

We arrived on September 4. The hotel was comfortable, but more important, Little Inge was there waiting for me, as was Wolfgang Mönninghoff, the director of publicity for Hoffmann und Campe. This was a gesture of generosity on the part of the publisher. The representatives of the Anne Frank Trust arriving from Basel included Claire Gysin-Morgenstern and her husband; Dr. Frank-Steiner, the head of the trust, and his wife; and the actor Buddy Elias, Anne's cousin and last surviving relative. I learned that the trust had been established in 1966 by Anne's now deceased father Otto "for the purpose of promoting charitable, social, and cultural work in memory of Anne Frank and to spread her message."

An exhibit in the nearby Westerse Church entitled "The World of Anne Frank," which has since been shown in many cities throughout the world, had just opened. Naturally we went to see it, though we didn't stay long. It was late in the afternoon, our first in Amsterdam. We were tired after the exhausting trip and felt drawn to 263 Prinsengracht, where the Franks' hiding place was located.

Since my ability to give architectural descriptions is minimal, I will quote that given by Ernst Schnabel in his book *Anne Frank: Spur eines Kindes* (*The Footsteps of Anne Frank*).[1] The text in quotation marks is taken from Anne's diary:

> *It is a narrow old brick building. . . . The front . . . has that quiet beauty which can be observed in so many of these old houses in Amsterdam. It comes from the perfect simplicity and the finely balanced proportions. . . .*
>
> *Aside from the door to the warehouse, the building has two narrow entrances. One of these, which was usually kept closed even when Frank still worked*

in the firm, leads to a small staircase that goes straight up to the second story, as is frequently the case in Dutch buildings. It is a steep, dangerous staircase. Behind the other door is a side entrance to the warehouse, and an ordinary staircase. "There is another door at the top of the stairs, with a frosted glass window in it, which has 'Office' written in black letters across it." The word can still be read. . . . The room is empty now and seems almost a small public hall.

Having heard about the Franks' hiding place, countless people make the pilgrimage to the building in which it is housed. And like us, they manage to negotiate the "steep, dangerous staircase." Following in "the footsteps of this child" turned out to be a very painful experience. As I looked at the pitiful little picture postcards pasted on the wall—of film stars, for instance—my heart sank. I remembered the fun we used to have at that age, collecting and exchanging photos of our favorite matinee idols. Filled with hope, Anne had taken these little tokens of happiness with her when she went into hiding. Among the comments we found in the open visitors' book there were both muted and piercing cries of despair, rage, sadness, and bewilderment; many visitors were trying in some way to vent their feelings. Here we were at the scene of a crime that practically the whole world is familiar with just because a bright little girl was planning to write a book of stories—*The Secret Annex.*[2] First came the diary, though—and then the German police.

What made me reflect further on our visit, aside from what had motivated us to go in the first place, was seeing my friend Ruth G.—two years older than I, educated at a boarding school run by the Moravian Brothers, later a physical education student—standing in front of a wall where the newspaper *Der Stürmer,* a Nazi weekly published by the notorious Jew-baiter Julius Streicher, had once been advertised in a showcase display. I could see that she was crying, and I heard her whisper, "I really didn't know."

To us who were openly discriminated against and marginalized for years, this was quite incomprehensible. And yet there are people whose memories work in strange ways. And there are people, like my friend, whose selective memories should be given the benefit of the doubt.

In reading about the house on Prinsengracht, I discovered that after the Franks' hiding place had been betrayed to the Germans (who betrayed them remains a mystery) and they and the others who had been hiding in the Secret Annex were deported, the building was left empty for so long that by 1957 there were plans to demolish it.

It was saved only by the establishment of the Anne Frank Foundation in Amsterdam.

All the photographs of Anne show her smiling. Ernst Schnabel included a wonderful dedication in his book: "For my children—that they may know."

Incidentally, to get from the hotel to the awards ceremony, I took a streetcar, something I hadn't done in thirty years.

"Look, we can't get out of this," Claire had said, "and didn't you say that you feel safe in a taxi? We can get off the streetcar whenever it makes a stop; there are taxis all over the place."

It wasn't easy for me—but we didn't have to get off. I *wanted* to get better. . . . On the return trip, though, I did treat myself to a relaxing taxi ride. And why not? I had barely arrived from Germany when I had had to face the prospect of an exciting but challenging day at the presentation ceremony.

Well, what do you say?" asked Little Inge as she slipped her arm through mine. "Isn't this an interesting street?" Yes, it was. It was also bewildering—townspeople and junkies, *provos* and tourists, a colorful mixture of races, all strolling down Kalverstraat. To remind myself of where I was, I glanced at the photograph of the crowd in the Merian guidebook on Amsterdam: yes, here I was right in the middle of it all, without a safe haven in sight. I began to feel a little uncomfortable. Fortunately, though, we seem to be inclined to remember the beautiful and exciting things in life.

Rows of chairs had been set up in the gallery facing the street. After the customary welcoming speeches, Efim Edkind, a literary historian who had been expelled from the USSR and was living in Paris, spoke in praise of the prizewinner Ida Fink. Her book *A Scrap of Time and Other Stories* describes Poland under German occupation.[3] Fink lived part of World War II in a ghetto and the other part in hiding. "Her stories are crafted in quiet words, free of sentimentality, tears, hatred, or vituperation," said Edkind. Later, when I read the stories, I thought to myself: In comparison to a life such as hers—spent in backrooms, barns, even in the forest; camouflaged, disguised, and forced to assume different identities—my experiences seem trivial indeed.

The speech in which Mrs. Fink expressed her gratitude for the award reflected in words what one could read on her face, that in spite of the unspeakably infernal past, she had remained a tolerant human being. The opportunity to meet her made me very happy. All of us were grateful to the selection committee for having discovered *A Scrap of Time* from among the myriad books on the Holocaust.

We received our certificates of award from Mayor van Thijn of Amsterdam. I have to admit that I felt both honored and delighted at having been awarded a prize named after Anne Frank.

That evening we were invited to a dinner given by the municipal administration. We were enchanted by the nostalgic ambience of the Keyser Restaurant on Baerlestraat— the dark wood paneling, the arches, and the alcoves; the soft lighting, the flecks of gold on the walls, and the many pictures. Now that the most emotional part of the evening was over, the guests felt more relaxed and at ease. I got to know Fritzi Frank, Anne's father's second wife. In a speech to the assembled guests, Alexander Ramati thanked the Anne Frank Trust on behalf of the recipients of the Recognition Award. We owe him a great debt of gratitude for his book *The Assisi Underground*, which is not widely enough known.[4] Ramati was one of the first war correspondents to enter Assisi in 1943 after the Wehrmacht had been forced to evacuate the town. He recounted the true story of Padre Rufino, the Franciscan priest who had been instructed by Bishop Nicolini to take 300 Jewish refugees under his personal protection. The refugees were subsequently entrusted to the care of the Order of St. Clare (Poor Clares) and later sent to Florence in a dramatic escape to keep them out of harm's way. From Florence they were able to reach the seaport of Genoa. Ramati has described for us the efforts of some incredibly brave human beings who often had to pay with their lives for their courageous acts. Incidentally, a Colonel Müller—a doctor, a Catholic, and the German commanding officer in Assisi—purposely did nothing to stop the rescue mission; in the film version of the book he was played by James Mason.[5] The movie is, unfortunately, not particularly well known; in March 1986 it played in Freiburg during Brotherhood Week and went almost unnoticed.

It wasn't until the following morning that we were able to talk to Klaus-Peter Wolf, the third prizewinner and the youngest of us all. We asked him why he had disappeared so suddenly the evening before.

"I wanted some *action*," the young gentlemen said, "so I took a cab to the Chinatown section."

"Beg your pardon?"

"That's what the taxi driver said, too. At night, he told me, I'd better stay away from places like that. But I explained to him that I was quite familiar with those kinds of districts."

The young author gave us an impressive description of where his literary interests lay. He wanted to tell the story of fringe groups and the disadvantaged. At the presentation ceremony he was honored for his novel about an asylum seeker.[6] His detailed descriptions of locales that were foreign to us and often colorful provided the makings for some very lively breakfast conversation. When I ran into him in October at the Frankfurt Book Fair, he was rushing off to an exhibit of young-adult books, where I am certain he charmed his audience.

Amsterdam was an unforgettable experience, but it once again raised the question of how to cope with the fact that the *wonderful* things we were enjoying now were somehow the result of horrible events that had taken place in the past.

1. Ernst Schnabel, *Anne Frank: Spur eines Kindes: ein Bericht* (Frankfurt am Main: Fischer Taschenbuch, 1958). [*Anne Frank: A Portrait in Courage* (New York: Harcourt, Brace and World, 1958). Published in Great Britain under the title *The Footsteps of Anne Frank* (London: Longmans, 1958).—TRANS.]

2. Anne Frank, *Anne Frank's Tales from the Secret Annex* (New York: Bantam Books, Washington Square Press, 1983).

3. Ida Fink, *A Scrap of Time and Other Stories*, trans. from the Polish by Madeline Levine and Francine Prose (New York: Pantheon Books, 1987).

4. Alexander Ramati, as told by Rufino Niccacci, *The Assisi Underground: The Priests Who Rescued Jews* (New York: Stein and Day, 1978). Published in Great Britain under the title *While the Pope Kept Silent: Assisi and the Nazi Occupation* (London: Allen and Unwin, 1978).

5. *The Assisi Underground*, prod. Menahem Golan and Yoram Globus, dir. Alexander Ramati, 115 min., Cannon Films, 1985, videocassette.—TRANS.

6. Klaus-Peter Wolf, *Die Abschiebung, oder Wer tötete Mahmut Perver?* (Zurich: Benzinger, 1984).

THE "RACIAL ASSESSMENT" OF M. B.

IN SEPTEMBER 1987, former Jewish residents of the town of Müllheim in the Markgräfler Land were invited to visit this former county seat. A very active and committed citizens' group made up of members of the younger generation was experimenting with different ways of exploring recent local history as reflected in historical documents and "rescuing the murder and other victims of that period from permanent anonymity and the indignity of being forgotten." Rolf Schuhbauer, the vice principal of Müllheim's high school, was working on a book in which he sought to trace the ordeals and sufferings of Müllheim's Jews during the Third Reich; it was published in 1988.[1] I was slated to give a reading in Müllheim the week the Holocaust survivors were scheduled to visit the city. At the same time, another survivor, a gentleman who was living in Müllheim and was deeply moved when he learned of our common experiences, emerged from the darkness of anonymity. M. B., as I shall call him, grew up in Freiburg.

231

M. B. was the son of a Christian father and a Jewish mother who had converted to Catholicism. After my reading was over, we were sitting in the company of the citizens' group when he began to talk about his life, the first time he had done so in forty-three years. His account turned out to be quite an adventure story. He survived because he had dared to take the existential leap, quite literally—right through the bolted window of a railway car that was crossing the Swiss Rhineland between the German towns of Weil and Grenzach (near Basel). I got dizzy just listening to him. Having risked his life and suffered serious injuries as a result, he managed to reach freedom. Although he wished to write his own account of his experiences, he agreed to let me publish one of the noteworthy documents in his possession, one that I felt would complement the letter I had received from Dr. O. in Weil am Rhein. In that letter Dr. O. had mentioned something that was beyond my ken at the time: "We—that is, my wife, who is 'only one-quarter Jewish,' and I, a 'pure-blooded Aryan'—were married in 1940; however, we had to submit beforehand to a series of degrading examinations—which we passed—to determine our 'racial makeup.'"

M. B. possessed documentation to clarify exactly what Dr. O. was referring to.

"I was determined to go to university," he wrote. "However, I was barred from attending." M. B. was aware that there was still a slender chance of being admitted. But in subjecting himself to the already degrading application process, he also had to obtain, among other things, a "ruling on observable racial characteristics" by the Racial Policy Office of the NSDAP, based on a racial assessment submitted by the Anthropological Institute of the University of Kiel on February 24, 1941:

Upon consultation with the Racial Policy Office of the NSDAP, M. B., a resident of Kiel-Ellerbeck, presented himself on February 18, 1941, for a racial assessment in order to obtain a final ruling on his application for permission to attend university.

The aggregate results of the racial examination are as follows:

B. is of medium height (167 cm.), has a narrow head and a cephalic index of 76.8 (the ratio of the breadth to the length of the skull). The shape of his head may therefore be described as of the mesocephalic type, placing him a few points below the mean in our province. The measurement and subsequent analysis of the minimum breadth of the forehead, the bizygomatic breadth (zygion to zygion), and the breadth of the jaw (gonion to gonion) indicate a face that is of medium width and, given its length, is most closely related to that of the Dalo-Nordic racial type.[2]

Hair color corresponds to the letter M on the chromatic scale and falls somewhere between blond and light brown. Eye color is blue (2a on the scale) and shows no evidence of granulations in the medium layer of the iris and hence no shades of brown.

Hair form and texture coarse, forehead high and slightly retreating, eyes deep-set, fold of the upper eyelid marked: eyebrows slightly curved and beginning to meet in the middle.

Nasal bridge straight, base of the nose upturned.

Upper lip straight, mouth small, lips full but not everted.

Facial form roughly pentagonal, lateral lines only slightly convergent, protruding chin, narrow when viewed from the front, somewhat angular.

Ears show no particular racial traits or charac-
teristics. M. B.'s observable racial characteristics are
largely in keeping with the phenotype of the Dalo-
Nordic race. Of course, in an examination such as this
in which we are precluded from covering further
details, we cannot state unequivocally whether it can
be assumed that the examinee has any recessive racial
traits. However, there is no reason to presume the
presence of a significant alien racial component, since
it would obviously be manifested in the examinee's
observable features.

Therefore, the question as to whether the observ-
able characteristics of the examinee exhibit any fea-
tures associated with the Near Eastern or any other
type of alien race can be answered unambiguously [in
the negative] to the degree that such racial character-
istics are not visibly detectable.

"None of us came from a region which, according to
Nazi racial 'doctrine,' was considered a habitat of the
'Dalo-Nordic race,'" this so-called "half-breed with no
observable alien racial characteristics" explained to me.
"Incidentally, I've sometimes wondered if the person who
performed the examination wasn't trying to help me pass by
using all that racist gibberish. All I know for certain is that
I was very fortunate."

As chance would have it, after I had finished reading the
"racial assessment" of this blue-eyed "half-breed," I was
handed a book entitled *Jugend unter Hitler* (*Youth under
Hitler*),[3] where I found references to Ernst Hiemer's *Der
Giftpilz* (*The Toadstool*),[4] a children's book published in
1938. In the book a teacher named Brinkmann, using lavish

234

visual aids, is shown instructing a boys' seventh-grade class; he has prepared a lesson in anthropology specifically designed for these stalwart young Germans.

You can tell Jews by their lips. They usually have thick lips. And their lower lip is often pendulous. Their eyelids are usually heavier and fleshier than ours. The look in their eyes is shifty and penetrating. You can tell by their eyes that they are deceitful and given to lying.

The lesson ends with all the children reading aloud the following maxim: "In the face of every Jew you can see the devil peeking through."

There were doubtless other teachers like Herr Brinkmann —and many children who put their faith in them. . . . Then I got this despairing letter from a woman in Freiburg, a committed Christian:

I ask myself whether I would have had the moral strength in those days to resist and help my Jewish fellow citizens. It's so easy to answer in the affirmative now. . . . I thank you with all my heart for your book; I only wish that it never had to have been written.

NOTES

1. Rolf Schuhbauer, *"Nehmt dieses kleine Heimatstück."* *Spuren und Stationen der Leidenswege von Müllheimer Juden zwischen 1933 und 1945* (Baden: Herausgegeben von der Stadt Müllheim, 1988).

2. Nazi racial doctrine taught that the following races exist-ed in Europe: Nordic (*nordisch*), Dalo-Nordic (*fälisch*), Mediterranean (*westisch*), Dinaric (*dinarisch*), Alpine (*ostisch* or *alpin*), and East-Baltic (*ostbaltisch*).—TRANS.

3. Heinz Boberach, *Jugend unter Hitler, Fotografierte Zeitgeschichte* (Dusseldorf: Droste Verlag, 1982).

4. Ernst Hiemer, *Der Giftpilz, ein Stürmerbuch für Jung und Alt: Erzählungen, Bilder von Fips* (Nuremberg: Verlag Der Stürmer, 1938).—TRANS.

MY WANDERINGS
THROUGH THE
BRANDENBURG MARCH

THE TIME HAS COME to explain how I came by those friends in Brielow who—as I mentioned at the beginning of this book—took me to Grosse Hamburgerstrasse after I hadn't been there for fifty years. . . .

In March 1987, I was supposed to give a talk at the Evangelical Academy of Müllheim an der Ruhr as part of a conference entitled "Ancient Magic—New Faith— Today's Witches." The title of my paper was "Why They Were Burned at the Stake: Thoughts on the Persecution of Witches by Church and Society." The year I gave my talk coincided with the five-hundredth anniversary of the publication of *Der Hexenhammer* (1487), a manual for witch-hunters by the two Dominican monks Institoris and Sprenger.[1] In 1977 I had published a book entitled *In tausend Teufels Namen—Hexenwahn am Oberrhein* (*In Heaven's Name: Witchcraft Hysteria in the Rhine River Valley*) that examined the historical obsession with witches in the Rhine River Valley; it was dedicated to "the memory of my father who fell victim to *our* century's obsession."[2]

At the conference there was a speaker from the former German Democratic Republic, Pastor Hans Ullrich Schulz from Potsdam. He had come as a representative of the School Department of the Evangelical Church of Berlin-Brandenburg. His paper—"Christianity between Idealism and Materialism: The Evangelical Church's Work with Schools and Students in the GDR"—had nothing to do with the theme of the conference.

And since the subject of his talk was of no particular interest to me and his was supposed to be the last paper presented at the conference, my friend Ruth and I had planned to leave a little early to prepare for a reading I was to give in the town of Voerde, not far from Freiburg. Thomas Heydrich, the speaker scheduled for the first evening, was slated to give a talk on "Witches in Theater, Art, and Literature through Songs and Stories," and I was very much looking forward to hearing him read his paper. Heydrich, however, was a no-show; he had gotten his dates mixed up, and as a result, he helped change my life. The pastor from Brandenburg was substituted for Heydrich that evening, and I found his talk so fascinating that I gave him a copy of my book. The next morning, he said that I simply had to come to the GDR to give a reading to his students and tell them about my life. "That's impossible," I said. The complicated and nerve-racking formalities you have to go through in order to cross the border would only cause me a great deal of anxiety. Later, while the conference

238

attendees were saying their formal farewells to each other, the pastor and the gentleman who had told the witch stories took a seat on either side of me. They enveloped me in a thick cloud of blue pipe smoke as they tried to persuade me that there was no reason to be afraid of crossing the border; nobody would touch a hair on my head—on the contrary, I would be welcomed with open arms.

In January 1988 I received the following letter from the youth pastor of the province of Brandenburg:

[S]eeing that you had such a satisfactory meeting with our colleague Pastor Schulz, we would like to issue you a cordial invitation to read from your books and talk about your life at one of our youth meetings—the upcoming student conference to be held May 6-8, 1988. The year 1988—the fiftieth anniversary of the pogrom against German Jews staged by the NSDAP—is an occasion for us to think about the Jewish legacy that informs our Christian faith. Since we have been asked to find eyewitnesses to the event, we would be delighted if you would accept our invitation. Please consider yourself a guest of the Youth Department of the Evangelical Church of Berlin-Brandenburg. The members of the Student Section will do their utmost to make sure that all your needs are met.

I vacillated between feelings of gratefulness (for the trust that had been reposed in me) and doubt. Many students in the former GDR had no chance to choose freely their own course of study or their profession. They were forced to do what the people "at the top" decided for them. Did I have a right to share my experiences with these students, considering they had taken place over forty years ago and that I was coming from a country in which any student could study whatever he or she wished? Not to mention the fact I was frightened of uniforms, of the frozen faces of the Volkspolizisten (People's Police), and of being stopped at the border for no reason at all. It was common knowledge that such things did in fact happen.

One stroke of good fortune in my life was having a friend in Freiburg like Rosemarie, a doctor who originally came from Leipzig. Several times a year she would travel to visit her father in East Germany.

"I'll drive you to the conference, go on to see my father, and pick you up on my way back," she said as she got out her pocket-size appointment book.

"Rosemarie," I said, "whenever I'm alone somewhere, I still get attacks of agoraphobia. Look, you know I have to hold on to your apron strings whenever I'm in transit. And now you tell me you're going to drop me off and then drive on to Leipzig."

"So what," said my doctor friend, quite unperturbed, "You're a seasoned traveler, and according to everything you've told me about Pastor Schulz, he should be perfectly able to provide you with an acceptable pair of apron strings. Seriously, though, you have a moral obligation to accept the invitation. And if you keep telling yourself that, you'll manage just fine."

In the meantime, Herr Schulz had moved on from his position as school pastor[3] in Potsdam to become the parish pastor in the village of Brielow, where he was entrusted with the care of the souls in several small parishes in the surrounding area of what I refer to as "Fontane country." In answer to my acceptance, I received a letter that quite overwhelmed me—they were absolutely delighted that I was coming.

We set off during the sunniest part of May. At the border crossing I saw firsthand what until then I had seen only on television: watchtowers, barbed wire, and officials with police dogs. Our ID cards were dispatched pneumatically through long metal tubes; sharp eyes checked to make sure that we resembled the photographs in our passports. All the same, we had no trouble crossing, even though I was carrying a parcel full of paperbacks that I intended to give to the local parish: forty copies of *Invisible Walls*.

When we reached the Havel, I naturally thought of Fontane. The only knowledge I had of the river was what I had read in his *Wanderungen durch die Mark Brandenburg* (*Wanderings through the Brandenburg March*):

> *The Havel is an unusual river; judging by its shape, you might call it the North German Neckar or the lowland Neckar. Coming from the north and ultimately flowing north again, it describes a semicircle; anyone who remembers the primitive swings of childhood days consisting of a rope suspended between two apple trees can easily visualize the curved line by which the Havel is depicted on our maps. Its blue waters and myriad bends (it is really a string of lakes) make it unique in a way. The little piece of earth that it embraces, our Havelland, was the site of the first civilized life in this part of the country. Right here, along the banks of the river, the bishoprics of Brandenburg and Havelberg were erected.*

We were on the western side of the "suspended rope," that is, the western part of the Havelland, where the little village of Brielow is situated, with its attractive rectory close to the church that is kept lit at night. It was the illuminated steeple that welcomed us. When we were greeted by the Schulz family, I knew instantly that after Rosemarie—my "imprinting object," as it were—had gone on to Leipzig the next day, I would feel perfectly secure in the rectory. "We're expecting a visit from friends in our sister parish," said the pastor (whom I soon started calling Uli), as his wife, Susanne, disappeared into the kitchen, apparently to prepare "a big spread." When their friends arrived, there was a great deal of surprise at first—they were from Baden, and we already knew each other.

On the evening of May 5, I read from *Invisible Walls* in the church hall of the Brielow rectory and related the story of my life. I presented the forty paperbacks (donated by the publisher) to an audience whose gratefulness almost embarrassed me; there were enough copies for Uli's fellow clergymen from the neighboring parishes as well. Now I understood: it didn't matter that books in the GDR were generally in plentiful supply and cheap; *whenever* a printing appeared, it instantly sold out.

ORANIENBURG/SACHSENHAUSEN

"Uli," I said the next morning, "I noticed on the map that Oranienburg is quite close to here."

"Do you really want to go there?"

I didn't know if I really *wanted* to go; I just felt I *had* to go. What my father had been forced to endure under nothing less than hellish conditions, I could surely endure in the sheltered environment provided by my friends.

For about an hour we drove through the sandy

Brandenburg Marches in Uli's Trabi, an East German car which, given his size and build, was quite cramped and uncomfortable.

> *The site chosen for the building of the concentration camp was located in a pine forest on the outskirts of Oranienburg, along the road to Schmachtenhagen near the lock at Lake Lehnitz. The camp was built in the shape of an equilateral triangle. Initially, the prisoners' camp, the Kommandantur (for camp officials), an industrial area and camp workshops measured some thirty-one hectares, which, with the building of compounds for the SS in subsequent years, increased to approximately 126 hectares. When the camp was liberated in 1945, it covered an area of 388 hectares.*

I obtained the aforementioned data from a brochure published by the East Germans.[4] In 1938, when the camp filled up after the pogrom of November 9, the number of barracks increased to seventy-seven. In June, "6,000 Gypsies, idlers, vagrants," previously convicted criminals, and so forth had been sent to the camp. They were followed by the victims of Kristallnacht, the "Night of Broken Glass."

Before I realized it, I was standing in infamous roll-call square and looking into the barracks and cramped cells. There was a camp museum in the former prisoners' kitchen. I was deathly afraid I might come across a photograph with my father's picture on it—until I told myself that he had, after all, come back alive from this place.

Uli managed to find some flowers, red tulips. I laid them on one of the bunks in barracks 7. It was labeled "Jewish Inmates" on the map of the camp. The documentation reads:

> *[A]pproximately 6,000 of them have been sent to Sachsenhausen concentration camp, where they have been exposed to the cold without any protective clothing. Those arriving include well-known artists, scientists, businessmen, and workers. . . .*

"Exposed to the cold without any protective clothing"—though my father had told us a lot at the time about the methods of tortures used in the camp, this was one of the few I actually mentioned in my book.

The Nationale Mahn- und Gedenkstätte Sachsenhausen (Sachsenhausen National Memorial) contained a series of stained-glass windows, in luminous colors, showing scenes of the suffering that had been endured in the camp. Each nation that had been attacked by the Nazi armies between 1939 and 1945 had its own room. There was also a space dedicated to the memory of the Warsaw Ghetto, which I was particularly gratified to see, because usually when the East Germans referred to these kinds of memorials, they spoke of "anti-Fascists" rather than the racially persecuted.

Twice we encountered a group of student visitors. One group consisted mainly of older students who weren't particularly interested in this obligatory "lesson at the scene of the crime." The other, younger group, however, was deeply moved by what they had seen and stood in a circle around their teacher animatedly asking questions.

In Fontane's *Wanderungen* I read the following:

> *The Havel then reveals itself near Oranienburg, the place we plan to wander through today. The road to*

Oranienburg passes by [the village of] Tegel and comes to a temporary halt at the romantic Sand Jug Tavern. Another hour and a half's trek takes us past spruce trees and more villages until we stop at a place laid out like a big city, with a magnificent rainbow arching overhead. This is the site of the palace. The weather clears up; the sun comes out. The building that is supposed to accommodate us is nearly hidden by the lindens surrounding it and confirms, among other things, our most favorable preconceptions, especially when we learn that it is both the town hall and a guest house. It is comforting to be in a place where justice and hospitality dwell in such close proximity to each other.

Never again will anybody be able to think such thoughts here. Our nineteenth-century wanderer could certainly never have imagined what very different thoughts must have gone through people's minds after 1933—any more than my father could have when he was a boy. My grandfather Jac Hecht, after all, had a branch of his Hamburg antique business on Tauenzienstrasse in Berlin (the city of Theodor Fontane). And it would have been very strange indeed if this family, with its keen interest in literature, had not traveled in a carriage through the Brandenburg March to that very same guest house in Oranienburg as they followed the trail of a writer whose complete works graced the shelves of their personal library.

Uli lit up his pipe outside the camp, while Susanne and I remained at this awful yet historical site a little longer. Both of them were concerned about me the whole time; they tried their best to understand my situation and were at least as exhausted as I was. "And we can't even offer you a cup of coffee on your way home," said Uli. We were on the road for almost an hour without seeing a single place to stop and have a bite. The only eating place we came across along the highway was a tiny establishment in Bagow, a little village. At least they served ice cream. We took a seat on their minuscule balcony. At the place next door to the eatery, a family of storks put on a show for us as we relaxed and watched them scamper across the roof; storks are a common sight here on the meadows, lakes, and ponds. We finally got our coffee at the rectory—and Susanne had baked a delicious rhubarb cake as well.

As I write this in the spring of 1990, I feel it is incumbent on me to make a few comments about the date of November 9, since I had to relive it in a sense on this May 6 at Oranienburg. Elie Wiesel gave an interview to the *Spiegel* in January 1990 in which he expressed his fears about an expanded Germany:

> *I am in favor of freedom of movement. I am also in favor of freedom for Berlin, but I would like to have seen the chancellor or the mayor or anyone else on this memorable day say: Today is a very special day in more than one respect; perhaps there is a symbolic significance in this. November 9, after all, is also the date of the shameful Kristallnacht. Why wasn't there a moment of silence or reflection in honor of the victims? In any event, November 9, 1938, had already been forgotten or at least eclipsed by November 9, 1989. And I wonder: what else will be forgotten?*

As for me, I was invited to give readings in remembrance

of Kristallnacht even after November 9, 1989. All my hosts spoke to me about the *dual significance of this date*. What I discovered was that those who have a sense of responsibility with regard to Germany's past would never suppress the year 1938 when they rejoice about the year 1989. Nobody, however, is responsible for this particular "irony of history." We will always have to think about it and take heed. To close with the words of Elie Wiesel: "This liberation must not be allowed to result in an impairment of memory."

At Oranienburg, in roll-call square, outside the barracks, and at the scenes of unspeakable crimes, I had the same thoughts that Wiesel now expressed in words: "Let no nation, no person, no group, no conscience be allowed to forget: we have lived through these dreadful times; *all we have left is the memory.*"

And we must strive *with all due care* to explain this to future generations.

HIRSCHLUCH

In 1925 employees of the Berlin Youth Welfare Department bought a parcel of wasteland on the outskirts of Storkow near the Polish border for fifty thousand reichsmarks. All that the land had on it was a farmhouse and a little pond. The reason for the purchase was that, in 1924, the Reichstag had enacted legislation setting vacation periods for minors. However, since young people did not always know what to do in their free time, juvenile crime began to increase. The situation called for remedial measures. As a result, the "Hirschluch Society" was established. Cabins and cottages were built on the land to serve as youth hostels. The young people who came to spend their weekends there helped in the work of reforestation, planting pine

247

trees, and so forth. It was the heyday of the German Youth Movement of the 1920s; young people prayed, danced, and played together.

The name Hirsch-Luch (Hart-Marsh), which was first mentioned around the year 1200, was an inspiration to young Christians. "As the hart panteth after the water brooks, so panteth my soul after thee, O God" (Psalms 42:1).

After the land had been used in various different ways—in keeping with the changing course of events in German history—the Evangelical Church of Brandenburg acquired the property in 1945. In the GDR get-togethers for young people were called *Jugendrüsten* (meetings to prepare the young). I had been invited to one such *Jugendrüste*, the theme of which was "The Bible and the Jews."

This secluded complex situated in a little pine forest was very much to my liking. It brought back memories of the things I enjoyed when I went on hikes—the woods, the heath, the sand, and the atmosphere of the youth hostels. The program included a "Jewish evening." About seventy young people had come to participate. Not all of them came because they were particularly religious, but because in these surroundings they could breathe freely and hear something other than the constant sloganeering of the Free German Youth, the former East German youth organization. And they were grateful for anything offered to them that was of a spiritual nature.

We were given an explanation of Jewish customs, which in this case revolved mainly around the festival of Hanukkah, celebrated in December. I thought it was an original and charming notion that we each received a little

248

bag filled with nuts and a kind of dreidel that was marked on each of its four sides with a different Hebrew letter. We learned that this spinning top was used in a popular children's game of chance called *sevivon*, the Hebrew word for dreidel. Hanukkah is a postbiblical festival during which gifts are exchanged, mainly among children. The holiday commemorates the revolt of Judas Maccabeus against the Seleucid king Antiochus IV and the Maccabees' subsequent victory over the Seleucid armies that had sought to impose Hellenism on Judea (167–165 B.C.). Lights are kindled in memory of the rededication of the Second Temple of Jerusalem after its desecration earlier by the hellenizing Seleucid king.

"You're the first Jew we've ever met," said one of the girls. Then it dawned on me that young people here were studying biblical history without ever having seen a Jew.

"I can only help you 'halfway', though," I said, and then I explained the macabre Nazi system of classifying into "first-degree and second-degree half-breeds" those who were neither Jews nor Germans as defined in the first implementation ordinance of the Nuremberg Laws. "I was called a 'half-Jew' or 'half-Aryan.' If I were to apply this same system to the children of marriages between Catholics and Protestants, I would have to refer to them as either 'half-Catholics' or 'half-Protestants.' However, none of us felt back then like openly ridiculing even something as laughable as that. The reason I say this is that there were millions of Nazi supporters who didn't think such things were funny at all. These classifications had been devised by mature adults, and they were used all the time."

I was nevertheless able to make a concrete contribution to the theme of the evening by recalling the melody of a

Hanukkah song. We had a transliteration of the Hebrew text: *"Maoz Tzur yeshuati*—Rock of Ages, let our song / Praise Thy saving power."* Roland and Andreas, two music students from Freiburg, set to music the timid sounds I had dredged up from the recesses of my memory (and which I'm sure were not exactly correct); an hour later they were playing the song on their guitars. Hanukkah in May. . . .

How did I happen to come by that melody?

In my book I wrote about the time that my Protestant religious teacher at school found out I was "half-Jewish"— or "half-Aryan," if you will—how he then ignored me and how I in turn ignored him and stopped attending his class. My parents were a little unsettled by the resulting gap in my education. So I began going to the nearby synagogue on Oberstrasse with my Jewish classmates for instruction in the Jewish faith. It must have been during the week of Hanukkah, because all I remember about my attempt to familiarize myself with Judaism was that delightful melody and the first line of that lovely song.

In the evening I gave a reading from my book to an audience of young people who at the time were themselves living under an oppressive system. They listened to my presentation attentively and with what I felt was mounting interest. What surprised me was that after I had finished, they asked the same questions as the students in West Germany. In particular, they wanted to find out about the resurgence of neo-Nazism, which—though I didn't know it then—was also making itself felt in the GDR. We sat together talking for quite some time. Later, as I headed for bed in my little cubbyhole in our cabin—my private room on the ground floor, so to speak—with a little pine forest just outside my window, I felt very happy. In the old days, when we arrived at a youth hostel from Hamburg, fleeing "gray city walls," we felt as though we had left the everyday world far behind and could finally breathe freely and without fear. Here, where I no longer had to be afraid of the everyday world, and in Freiburg, which was "blessed by the sun" and where "gray city walls" weren't an issue, I felt as though the clock had been turned back a little to a happy time in my life, to a bit of the bright side of romanticism.

Early the next morning, we went to the little Jewish cemetery that was maintained by the village of Starkow. The pastors were able to decipher some of the Hebrew inscriptions on the weathered headstones. For these young Christians, though, they were largely relics of a remote and vanished world. So I was all the more grateful to those in the School Department of the Evangelical Church in Brandenburg who had made the effort to take a fresh look at this chapter in German and Jewish history.

We had a leisurely breakfast so that everyone could say good-bye to each other as well as to me. A young man pulled me over to a long table. "This is the highest one— you'll be more comfortable here."

Then a girl said, "I heard you have a problem with our fatty sausage, so I rustled you up a soft-boiled egg. OK?"

I was deeply moved and replied, "OK." ("OK"—that terse affirmation you always hear in American movies and other forms of entertainment—had actually made its way to East Germany!)

Everybody showed up at breakfast with a specialty from home. This was my chance to reacquaint myself with a delicacy that, because of all the superdelicacies that were now available in West Germany, had long been forgotten, namely "cold dog," a dessert made of butter cookies piled in layers one on top of the other and held together with a mixture of cocoa and shortening. It is then refrigerated and served chilled. It tasted absolutely wonderful.

This Sunday was May 8, the anniversary of the liberation by the Allied armies. I was the only person present who had witnessed the event; everybody else was a member of the postwar generation. They asked me to tell them what I had experienced. At that time, we were living in the town of Staufen in Breisgau, at the western foot of the Black Forest, inside a granary on Marktplatz. Early that morning, we went to the grocery store so we could each buy ourselves a bottle of kirschwasser made by the world-famous Schladen distillery. I might not have remembered all this if it hadn't been for the fact that I was standing next to the wife of the branch leader of the local Nazi Party. She told me that her husband was firmly convinced that even now V-3s were being used [to shell London]. The V-3 was one of the so-called "miracle weapons" that the regime was promoting as a means to instill hope in those who daily saw with their own eyes what was really happening. No one dared yet to laugh out loud. The SS was still shelling our little town from nearby Münstertal. And people knew they would keep on killing wherever they gained a foothold. It seemed there was nothing but scorched earth and murdered human beings. During the final days in Münstertal a clergyman had been butchered. . . .

As we looked down from our window onto the main street, we saw dark-skinned Spahis,[5] part of the French army, approaching on horseback; in their long white coats, they looked almost as if they had stepped out of *The Arabian Nights.*

I wasted no time getting myself to Allied headquarters, where I pleaded with those in charge to take us with them part of the way if the SS invaded Staufen again and they were forced to withdraw. Fortunately, nothing of the sort came to pass.

Before we were all about to leave Hirschluch, I was given a list that I had sworn to take back home with me; seventy young people had written down their names and addresses and said they wanted to have a copy of my book. Friends in Freiburg and Hamburg, including the publisher, donated what was needed to make their wish come true— and in its own way so did the GDR customs service. After a few requests for additional particulars, they allowed the parcel to go through.

To me the replies I received from these young readers in Brandenburg, Potsdam, and Berlin, so hungry for historical literature, are among the most important I have collected.

At around the same time I got to know Isolde J., a teacher in Beelitz. In June 1989 she wrote me as follows:

There's an American film about the life of Anne Frank playing on East German television right now. How sorry I am again that I don't have a TV set. I know I'm going to feel very unhappy tonight.

Miep Gies's memoirs, *Anne Frank Remembered,* had been serialized in East German newspapers, and Frau J. had told me that she had saved every chapter as it was published.[6] I sent her a copy of the book. In her letter of thanks she told me that she and her young students had painted pictures to illustrate the events in the "Secret Annex" on Prinsengracht, just as they were described by Anne, and then displayed them on a bulletin board. "In the meantime, the children and I have seen the photos in the book. Sometimes I try to imagine what their faces looked like when they realized the magnitude of what had taken place."

THE GUILT FEELINGS OF IRENE L.

In August 1990 I received a letter from a native of Hamburg living in southern Germany. She had long been urged by her children to write down her experiences, but to no avail.

It's possible we may have met at one time. . . . My mother was Jewish, my father Aryan. They were not allowed to marry. . . . My sister was born in 1935, I in 1937. When I was not quite two years old, my mother was sent to Ravensbrück. My father was sentenced to prison for having sexual relations with a non-Aryan. He spent years in a penal camp in the Emsland moors near Lingen and ended up fighting in a rehabilitation battalion at the front. He was ultimately reported as missing in action. I always had guilt feelings, telling myself that I was at fault for my father's death because it was partly a result of my being born.

My sister was raised by my grandmother. I was sent to a Jewish orphanage. However, since there was a danger of the children being deported, the Jewish Community arranged for me to live in a foster home. My foster father was Jewish, my foster mother Aryan. I was four years old at the time. We lived at number 3 Rappstrasse near Grindel and Schlump. My new father was a musician, a bandleader; at one time he had taught violin and been a merchant seaman.

Unfortunately, something must have happened in that marriage to cause the Youth Welfare Office to have little Irene removed from her foster parents' care. It was a traumatic experience because she very much liked her foster father—and had just the opposite feeling for her new legal guardian.

I attended the middle school on Mittelweg. Hannelore Hoger, who had the lead in the film Die Bertinis, *was my schoolmate. I never had any school "friends."*

Since I grew up among adults, I find it difficult even now to form friendships. I've never seen Die Bertinis. *It is still hard for me to talk about those times; I am only gradually getting used to seeing films on the subject. When I talk with someone about those days, I sometimes begin to shake uncontrollably. I have suppressed the whole thing. Even now I'm afraid that it will start all over again, the persecution.*

Frau L. became a bookseller and then in 1971 went to night school to become a teacher.

> *My first husband, whom I married when I was twenty-four and penniless, was fifty-four and had been a Nazi. Marrying me must have been a way for him to make amends or something. He had been an SS man, had volunteered for the war, fought in Poland, Greece, under Rommel, been a POW, and returned home long after the war was over. . . .*
>
> *I worked in the office of an Evangelical parish. Originally we wanted to have children, but then he opposed the idea. He was afraid they might look Jewish (my mother had fairly dark hair). He died in 1972, and I remarried in 1977. . . . In 1979 I gave birth to a daughter; she is blond like my biological father.*

Irene's remembrances left me nearly breathless. Still I

255

believe that, blemishes and all, they are part of the vast unspeakable mosaic. I am grateful to Frau L. for putting her trust in me and granting me permission to pass on this particular variant of the "half-breed" story.

THE COURAGE OF MARTHA LANGER

One of my happiest moments was the time I met Ingeborg Langer, for in getting to know her, the past came full circle.

In my book I described how Jews were confined to their homes after dark and usually had to while away their last night in Germany in the Hotel Reichshof before their trains left the central station on the other side of the street—always dreading that the Gestapo might think up some way of preventing them from reaching freedom. In 1940 Little Inge and I had accompanied the Hechts—my father's brother Edgar, his wife, and their eight-year old son, Hänschen—to the hotel before they left for Shanghai. That is where we spent their final hours in Germany and said our good-byes to each other. At that time, we could not imagine, of course, that something good and courageous was happening in secret there: Frau Martha Langer had joined the Nazi Party to make sure she would always be considered "above suspicion." In the meantime, however, she had partitioned off a section of the hotel by erecting a wall and building a number of inaccessible rooms. Here she hid the threatened and the persecuted, supplying them with food and obtaining papers and money for them to emigrate. A tree is planted in her honor on the Avenue of the Righteous at Yad Vashem.

I wrote about this in my book, as a result of which I met

Martha's daughter-in-law Ingeborg. She continues to be deeply concerned about the fate of those who survived and arranged for me to give readings at a number of schools. She even tried—unsuccessfully—to have *Invisible Walls* performed onstage in Hamburg. When my brother Wolfgang was in Hamburg, she invited us and Ralph Giordano to visit her home in Othmarschen. I was already familiar with her magnificent estate from reading Erich Lüth's history of the family. And now here we were walking "in the parklike garden, a charming little wood planted with exotic trees and sprinkled with meadows on which this chronicler recently saw, aside from a few cows, a pony grazing and kicking up its heels."[7] One of the cows—or to use Lüth's term, a "Langer lawn mower"—had just given birth to a calf, and the pony was now joined by a horse. Here, where the traces of bomb craters still evoked old memories, Ralph Giordano pointed down to the riverbank and once again told the story that had made us catch our breath in the *Bertinis* about a power-crazed German and his dog chasing a frightened Jewish family away from the banks of the Elbe. Wolfgang and I, though, had more pleasant memories—of sailing happily past the riverbank, being taken aboard the boats of our "Aryan" friends, and spending many hours free of fear.

Everything here was so peaceful now. A few weeks before our get-together, Ingeborg Langer had written me from Israel:

Without being explicit, your book is more than a story of the evil that men do; it is also about the danger of nationalism and a nation's capacity for indifference. In my opinion, what is most important is to teach children always to be vigilant and not to remain indifferent whenever injustices are perpetrated.

The title of this chapter refers to the book *Wanderungen durch die Mark Brandenburg* (*Wanderings through the Brandenburg March*) by the Berlin novelist and critic Theodor Fontane (1819–98). It was based on a series of journeys through Prussia's Brandenburg March from 1859 to 1882 and appeared in four volumes, in 1862, 1863, 1873, and 1882.—TRANS.

1. Heinrich Institoris, *Der Hexenhammer*, Von Jakob Sprenger und Heinrich Institoris, Zum ersten Male ins Deutsche übertragen und eingeleitet, von J. W. R. Schmidt, 3 vols. (Berlin: H. Barsdorf, 1920). Translation into German of the original *Malleus maleficarum*.—TRANS.

2. Ingeborg Hecht, *In tausend Teufels Namen: Hexenwahm am Oberrhein* (Freiburg im Breisgau: Rombach, 1977).—TRANS.

3. According to Article 44 of the GDR's constitution of October 7, 1949, regarding religious instruction at school: "The right of the church to give religious instruction on school premises is guaranteed. Religious instruction is given by personnel selected by the church." Jan F. Triska, ed., *Constitutions of the Communist Party-States* (Stanford, Calif.: Hoover Institution on War, Revolution and Peace, 1968).—TRANS.

4. Lagerarbeitsgemeinschaft Sachsenhausen bei der Zentralleitung des Komitees der Antifaschistischen Widerstandskampfes der DDR, *Sachsenhausen* (Berlin: VEB Deutscher Verlag der Wissenschaften, 1974).

5. This is a term used for native Algerian horsemen serving under the French government.

6. Miep Gies, with Alison Leslie Gold, *Anne Frank Remembered: The Story of the Woman Who Helped to Hide the Frank Family* (New York: Simon and Schuster, 1987). The German translation was published in West Germany by the Scherz Verlag in Munich in 1987 and a short time later in the former GDR.

7. Erich Lüth, *Das Hotel Reichshof: eine Hamburger Familiengeschichte, 1910–1985* (Hamburg: Ernst Kabel Verlag, 1985).

Jewish Lives